Cambridge Elements

Elements in Philosophy and Logic
edited by
Bradley Armour-Garb
SUNY Albany
Frederick Kroon
The University of Auckland

HIGHER-ORDER LOGIC AND TYPE THEORY

John L. Bell
University of Western Ontario

CAMBRIDGE
UNIVERSITY PRESS

CAMBRIDGE
UNIVERSITY PRESS

University Printing House, Cambridge CB2 8BS, United Kingdom

One Liberty Plaza, 20th Floor, New York, NY 10006, USA

477 Williamstown Road, Port Melbourne, VIC 3207, Australia

314–321, 3rd Floor, Plot 3, Splendor Forum, Jasola District Centre, New Delhi – 110025, India

103 Penang Road, #05–06/07, Visioncrest Commercial, Singapore 238467

Cambridge University Press is part of the University of Cambridge.

It furthers the University's mission by disseminating knowledge in the pursuit of education, learning, and research at the highest international levels of excellence.

www.cambridge.org
Information on this title: www.cambridge.org/9781108986908
DOI: 10.1017/9781108981804

First published 2022

A catalogue record for this publication is available from the British Library.

ISBN 978-1-108-98690-8 Paperback
ISSN 2516-418X (online)
ISSN 2516-4171 (print)

Higher-Order Logic and Type Theory

Elements in Philosophy and Logic

DOI: 10.1017/9781108981804
First published online: March 2022

John L. Bell
University of Western Ontario

Author for correspondence: John L. Bell, jbell@uwo.ca

Abstract: This Element is an exposition of second- and higher-order logic and type theory. It begins with a presentation of the syntax and semantics of classical second-order logic, pointing up the contrasts with first-order logic. This leads to a discussion of higher-order logic based on the concept of a type. Section 2 contains an account of the origins and nature of type theory and its relationship to set theory. Section 3 introduces local set theory (also known as 'higher-order intuitionistic logic'), an important form of type theory based on intuitionistic logic. In Section 4, a number of contemporary forms of type theory are described, all of which are based on the so-called 'doctrine of propositions as types'. The Element concludes with an Appendix in which the semantics for local set theory – based on category theory – is outlined.

Keywords: logic, type, proposition, set, constructive

ISBNs: 9781108986908 (PB), 9781108981804 (OC)
ISSNs: 2516-418X (online), 2516-4171 (print)

Contents

1 Second- and Higher-Order Logic 1

2 Type Theory and Its Origins 15

3 Local Set Theory 31

4 Newer Forms of Type Theory Based on the Doctrine of 'Propositions as Types' 47

Appendix: The Semantics of Local Set Theory/ Intuitionistic Higher-Order Logic 63

Bibliography 75

1 Second- and Higher-Order Logic

Second-order logic is a form of logic in which the rules of statement formation permit quantification over relations and properties, in addition to the quantification over individuals allowed in first-order logic. Thus, for example, the statement

Napoleon won every battle he fought before Waterloo
is first-order, while the statement
Napoleon had all the properties of a great general
is second-order.

In *higher-order logic*, the idea underlying second-order logic is extended to embrace quantification over higher-order entities such as properties of properties and relations between relations.

1.1 The Syntax and Semantics of Second-Order Logic

The vocabulary on which second-order logic[1] is based is an extension of that of first-order logic. A typical vocabulary for first-order logic – a *first-order vocabulary* – consists of the following symbols:

- *(Individual) constant symbols a, b, c, …*
- *(Individual) variables x, y, z, …*
- *Relation symbols P, Q, …*. Each relation symbol is assigned a natural number $n \geq 1$ called its *multiplicity*. A relation symbol of multiplicity *n* will be called *n-ary*. A 1-ary relation symbol is called a *predicate symbol*
- *Function symbols f, g, h, …*. Each such symbol is assigned a number $n \geq 1$ called its *multiplicity*. An operation symbol of multiplicity *n* will be said to be *n-ary*. A 1- or 2-ary function symbol is called *unary* or *binary*
- *Logical operators* $\wedge$, $\vee$, $\neg$, $\rightarrow$, and $\leftrightarrow$
- *Quantifiers* $\exists$ and $\forall$
- *Equality symbol* =
- *Punctuation symbols* (,) and [,]

Relation symbols are also called *second-level constants*.

The *terms* of our logical vocabulary are now defined as follows:

(i) Any variable or name standing alone is a term.
(ii) If f is an n-ary operation symbol and $t_1, \ldots, t_n$ are n terms, then $f\,t_1 \ldots, t_n$ is a term.
(iii) Nothing is a term unless it follows from **(i)** and **(ii)** that it is so.

[1] Second-order logic first appears explicitly in Frege's *Begriffsschrift* (1879).

Formulas in a first-order vocabulary are defined as follows:

1. The following are formulas: **(i)** an n-ary relation symbol followed by n terms and **(ii)** any expression of the form $s = t$, where s and t are terms. These are known as *atomic* formulas.
2. If φ and ψ are formulas,[2] so are $\neg\varphi$, $\varphi \wedge \psi$ $\varphi \vee \psi$ $\varphi \rightarrow \psi$, and $\varphi \leftrightarrow \psi$.
3. If φ is a formula and x a variable, then both $\exists x\ \varphi$ and $\forall x\ \varphi$ are formulas. In each of these formulas, the (occurrence of the) variable is said to be *bound.* A(n) (occurrence of a) variable in a formula that is not bound is called *free.*
4. Nothing counts as a formula unless its being so follows from clauses **1** to **3**.

A *sentence* is a formula in which each variable is bound in the aforementioned sense. We write $s \neq t$ as an abbreviation for $\neg(s = t)$.

Clause **3** encapsulates the 'first-order' nature of a first-order vocabulary, for it licenses quantification over individual variables, which may be considered *first-level* entities. A *second-order vocabulary*, or a *vocabulary for second-order logic*, is an extension of a first-order vocabulary that also licenses quantification over *second-level* entities such as relations. To be precise, a second-order vocabulary is obtained by adding to a first-order vocabulary a collection of symbols $X, Y, Z, \ldots$ called *relations* or *second-level variables*.[3] Each relation variable is assigned a natural number $n \geq 1$ called its *multiplicity.* A relation variable of multiplicity n will be called *n-ary,* and a 1-ary relation variable is called a *predicate variable.* The formulas of a second-order vocabulary are defined by expanding clause **1(i)** to admit as a formula any n-ary relation variable followed by n terms and expanding clause **3** to admit as formulas $(\exists X)\varphi$ and $(\forall X)\varphi$ for any formula φ and relation variable X. Free and bound variables and sentences are defined as in the first-order case.

A second-order vocabulary may be considered as a *many-sorted* first-order vocabulary. In a many-sorted first-order vocabulary, one is given a collection of entities called *sorts*, and each variable or constant is assigned a particular sort. Quantification is then restricted to each sort. Thus, in a second-order vocabulary, the collection for each $n \geq 1$ of n-ary relation variables may be taken to constitute a separate sort and second-order quantification as first-order quantification over the relevant sort.

We proceed to describe the *semantics* of second-order logic. Roughly speaking, this is an extension of the semantics of first-order logic in which the relation variables are interpreted as *set-theoretic relations* over the domain of interpretation of the individual variables. In particular, predicate variables are interpreted as *subsets* of the domain of interpretation.

[2] We shall use lower-case Greek letters φ, ψ, α, β, γ to denote arbitrary formulas.

[3] A second-order vocabulary can also contain *function variables.* We shall not consider this possibility here.

We recall the semantics of first-order logic. This is based on the concept of a *structure.* Given a first-order vocabulary **L**, let us suppose for specificity that the individual variables of **L** are enumerated as a list $v_0, v_1, \ldots, v_n, \ldots$, that the relation symbols, function symbols, and individual constants of **L** are presented as indexed lists $(P_i, i \in I)$, $(f_j j \in J)$, $(c_k, k \in K)$, respectively, and that for each $i \in I$, $j \in J$, the multiplicities of P_i, f_j are the natural numbers $n(i)$, $m(j)$, respectively. Then an **L**-*structure* (also called an *interpretation* of **L**) is a triple

$$\mathfrak{A} = (A, \{R_i : i \in I\}, \{g_j : j \in J\}, \{e_k : k \in K\}),$$

where A, the *domain* or *universe* of $\mathfrak{A}$, is a *non-empty* set; $\{R_i : i \in I\}$ is an indexed family of relations on A, where, for each $i \in I$, R_i is $n(i)$-ary;[4] $\{g_j : j \in J\}$, is an indexed family of operations[5] on A, where each g_j is $m(j)$-ary; and $\{e_k : k \in k\}$ is an indexed set of elements of A – the *designated elements* of $\mathfrak{A}$. We call R_i, g_j, e_k the *denotations* of P_i, f_j, c_k, respectively, in $\mathfrak{A}$.

Now let $\mathbf{a} = (a_0, a_1, \ldots)$ be a countable sequence of elements of A (such a sequence will be referred to henceforth as an A-*sequence*). For any term t, we define its *interpretation* $t^{(\mathfrak{A},a)}$ *in* $(\mathfrak{A}, a)$ as follows:

(i) $c_k{}^{(\mathfrak{A},a)} = e_k$[6]
(ii) $v_n^{(\mathfrak{A},a)} = a_n$
(iii) For $j \in J$, terms $t_1, \ldots, t_{m(j)}$, $f_j t_1 \ldots t_{m(j)}^{(\mathfrak{A},a)} = g_j\left(t_1^{(\mathfrak{A},a)}, \ldots, t_{m(j)}^{(\mathfrak{A},a)}\right)$

For a natural number n and $b \in A$, we define

$$[n|\, b]\boldsymbol{a} = (a_0, a_1, \ldots, a_{n-1}, b, a_{n+1}, \ldots).$$

For a formula φ, we define the relation ***a*** *satisfies* φ *in* $\mathfrak{A}$,

$$\mathfrak{A} \models_a \varphi,$$

as follows:

1) for terms t and u,

$$\mathfrak{A} \models_a t = u \Leftrightarrow t^{(\mathfrak{A},a)} = u^{(\mathfrak{A},a)}$$

2) for terms $t_1, \ldots, t_{n(i)}$,

$$\mathfrak{A} \models_a P_i t_1 \ldots t_{n(i)} \Leftrightarrow R_i\left(t_1{}^{(\mathfrak{A},a)}, \ldots, t_{n(i)}^{(\mathfrak{A},a)}\right)$$

3) $\mathfrak{A} \models_a \neg\varphi \Leftrightarrow$ not $\mathfrak{A} \models_a \varphi$
4) $\mathfrak{A} \models_a \varphi \wedge \psi \Leftrightarrow \mathfrak{A} \models_a \varphi$ and $\mathfrak{A} \models_a \psi$

---

4 When $n(i) = 1$, R_i is a *property* defined on A, which may be identified with a *subset* of A.
5 An *n-ary operation* on a set A is a function $A^n = A \times \ldots \times A \to A$.
6 Thus, the interpretation of c_k in ($\mathfrak{A}$, a) is just its denotation in $\mathfrak{A}$.

5) $\mathfrak{A} \models_a \varphi \vee \psi \Leftrightarrow \mathfrak{A} \models_a \varphi$ or $\mathfrak{A} \models_a \psi$
6) $\mathfrak{A} \models_a \varphi \rightarrow \psi \Leftrightarrow$ if $\mathfrak{A} \models_a \varphi$, then $\mathfrak{A} \models_a \psi$
7) $\mathfrak{A} \models_a \varphi \leftrightarrow \psi \Leftrightarrow \mathfrak{A} \models_a \varphi$ if and only if $\mathfrak{A} \models_a \psi$
8) $\mathfrak{A} \models_a \exists v_n \varphi \Leftrightarrow$ for some $b \in A$, $\mathfrak{A} \models_{[n|\,b]a} \varphi$
9) $\mathfrak{A} \models_a \forall v_n \varphi \Leftrightarrow$ for all $b \in A$, $\mathfrak{A} \models_{[n|\,b]a} \varphi$

A formula φ is *true* in $\mathfrak{A}$ if $\mathfrak{A} \models_a \varphi$ for *every* A-sequence $\boldsymbol{a}$ and *satisfiable* in $\mathfrak{A}$ if $\mathfrak{A} \models_a \varphi$ for *some* A-sequence $\boldsymbol{a}$. For sentences, satisfiability and truth in a structure coincide. If a sentence σ is true in $\mathfrak{A}$, we write $\mathfrak{A} \models \sigma$ and call $\mathfrak{A}$ a *model* of σ. If $\mathfrak{A} \models \neg\sigma$, we say that σ is *false* in $\mathfrak{A}$. If Σ is a set of sentences of **L**, $\mathfrak{A}$ is a *model of* Σ, written $\mathfrak{A} \models \Sigma$, if each member of Σ is true in $\mathfrak{A}$. The sentence σ is a *(first-order) logical consequence of* Σ, written $\Sigma \models \sigma$, if σ is true in every model of Σ. σ is (logically) *valid* if $\emptyset \models \sigma$, that is, if σ is true in *every* interpretation of **L**.

Now the semantics of first-order logic is readily extended to second-order logic. Given a second-order vocabulary $\mathbf{L}'$ extending a first-order vocabulary **L**, we suppose that for each $n \geq 1$, the n-ary relation variables of $\mathbf{L}'$ are enumerated as a list $V_0^{(n)}, \ V_1^{(n)}, \ldots$. If A is a set, an L'*-sequence of relations on* A is a double sequence $\mathbf{R} = \left(R_m^{(n)} : m = 0,\ 1,\ \ldots\ n = 1,\ 2,\ \ldots\right)$ of relations on A such that for each n, $R_m^{(n)}$ is n-ary.

For a natural number n and an n-ary relation Q on A, we define $[m|Q]\boldsymbol{R}$ to be the result of replacing $R_m^{(n)}$ by Q in $\boldsymbol{R}$.

If $\mathfrak{A}$ is an **L**-structure and $\boldsymbol{R}$ an $\mathbf{L}'$-sequence of relations on A, we extend the notion of satisfaction to $\mathbf{L}'$-formulas by means of the rules (in which, for simplicity, we have suppressed reference to the A-sequence $\boldsymbol{a}$):

10) $\mathfrak{A} \models_{\boldsymbol{R}} \exists V_m^{(n)} \varphi \Leftrightarrow$ for some n-ary relation Q on A, $\mathfrak{A} \models_{[m|\,Q]\boldsymbol{R}} \varphi$
11) $\mathfrak{A} \models_{\boldsymbol{R}} \forall V_m(n) \varphi \Leftrightarrow$ for any n-ary relation Q on A, $\mathfrak{A} \models_{[m|\,Q]\boldsymbol{R}} \varphi$

Clauses 10 and 11 constitute the core of the idea of a *second-order interpretation.* Clause 11 in particular asserts that in a second-order interpretation, a universal second-order quantifier '$\forall X$' is understood to mean 'for *all* relations or subsets X of the domain'.

The notions of truth, satisfiability model, and logical consequence then extend automatically to second-order sentences.

1.2 The Expressive Power of Second-Order Logic: Second-Order Arithmetic

Second-order logic has vastly more expressive power than first-order logic. For example, students of mathematical logic soon come to learn that the property of having a finite domain is not expressible in first-order terms, that is, there is no set Σ of first-order sentences such that the models of Σ are precisely the structures with finite domains. By contrast, the property of having a finite domain can be expressed by the single second-order sentence as follows:

Fin $\forall X[[\forall x\exists!yX(x,y)\wedge\forall x\forall y\forall z[X(x,y)\wedge X(z,y)\rightarrow x=z]\rightarrow\forall y\exists xX(x,y)]]$,

where X is a binary relation variable and $\exists!y\varphi(y)$ is an abbreviation for the sentence $\exists y\forall x[\varphi(x)\leftrightarrow x=y]$, which expresses 'there is a unique y such that $\varphi(y)$'. Thus, **Fin** says that 'any binary relation which is the graph of an injective function of the domain into itself is surjective'. And this holds if and only if the domain is finite.

Second-Order Arithmetic. Mathematical concepts are often presented by means of *postulates* (sometimes called *axioms*) formulated as sentences of first- or second-order logic. In writing such sentences, it is customary to place binary operation symbols between arguments rather than in front of them: thus, for example, one writes $x+y$ instead of $+xy$.

The logical vocabulary for *arithmetic* includes a unary function symbol s, two binary function symbols $+$ and $\times$, and an individual constant 0. The *standard interpretation* $\mathfrak{N}$ of this vocabulary is the structure based on the familiar *natural number system*, specified as follows:

domain of $\mathfrak{N}$: the set $N=\{0,1,2,\ldots\}$ of natural numbers
denotation in $\mathfrak{N}$ of s: the (immediate) successor operation $\bullet\ +\ 1$ on N
denotations in $\mathfrak{N}$ of $+$ and $\times$: the usual operations of addition and multiplication on N
denotation in $\mathfrak{N}$ of *0*: the natural number zero

The domain and successor operation of the standard interpretation may be represented by the following *diagram*:

$(*)\quad 0\rightarrow\mathbf{1}\rightarrow 2\rightarrow 3\rightarrow\ \ldots$

in which each arrow proceeds from an element to its successor.
The postulates for *basic first-order arithmetic* (**BFOA**) are the following:

B1 $\forall x\forall y(x\neq y\rightarrow sx\neq sy)$
B2 $\forall x\ \ 0\neq sx$
B3 $\forall x(x\neq 0\rightarrow\exists y(x=sy))$
B4 $\forall x\ \ x+0=x$
B5 $\forall x\forall y\ x+sy=s(x+y)$
B6 $\forall x\ \ x\times 0=0$
B7 $\forall x\forall y\ \ x\times sy=(x\times y)+x.$

Each of these postulates is true in $\mathfrak{N}$. The first three express familiar facts about the successor operation:

B1 *Distinct natural numbers have distinct successors.*
B2 *Zero is the successor of no natural number.*
B3 *Every non-zero natural number is a successor.*

The next two postulates tell us how to add in this notation:

B4 *Adding 0 has no effect.*
B5 $(x + y) + 1 = x + (y + 1)$.

In this notation, each *numeral* 1, 2, 3, 4, … is represented by a string of s's of the appropriate length followed by 0, as in

$$1 = s0 \; 2 = ss0 \; 3 = sss0 \; 4 = ssss0, \ldots.$$

BFOA has a property known as *incompleteness*, which means that there are certain sentences true in the standard interpretation $\mathfrak{B}$ that are *not (first-order) logical consequences* of **BFOA** or are, simply, *independent* of **BFOA**. For instance, although each of the sentences

$$0 \neq s0, s0 \neq ss0, ss0 \neq sss0, \ \ldots$$

is a logical consequence of **BFOA**, the corresponding generalization

(a) $\forall x \; x \neq sx$

is *not*. Similarly, *none* of the following generalizations is a logical consequence of (**BFOA**), though each of their particular instances is:

(b) $\forall x \quad 0 + x = x$
(c) $\forall x \forall y \forall z \quad x + (y + z) = (x + y) + z$
(d) $\forall x \forall y \quad x + y = y + x$
(e) $\forall x \quad 0 \times x = 0$
(f) $\forall x \forall y \quad sx \times y = (x \times y) + y$
(g) $\forall x \forall y \quad x \times y = y \times x$

To establish the independence of (a)–(g) from the postulates of **BFOA**, we must supply a model of **BFOA**, that is, an interpretation in which **B1–B7** are true, but in which (a)–(g) are *false*. It is not difficult to check that the following interpretation $\mathfrak{B}$ does the job:

domain of $\mathfrak{B}$: the set of natural numbers together with two additional distinct objects \$ and @ *denotation of s*: indicated by the following diagram, in which each arrow leads from a member of the domain to its successor:

(**)

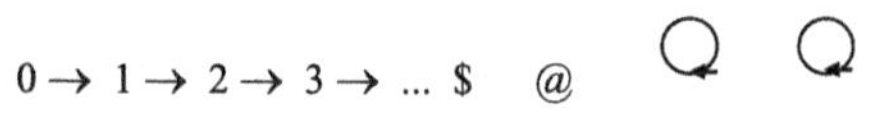

denotations of $+$ and $\times$: these are as usual when the arguments are both natural numbers. When one or both arguments is/are \$ or @, the values are given by the following tables, in which n is any natural number and $n^{>}$ is any non-zero natural number:

+	***n***	**\$**	**@**
N		@	\$
\$	\$	@	\$
@	@	@	\$

×	**0**	***n***$^{>}$	**\$**	**@**
n	0	\$	@	
\$	0	@	@	@
@	0	\$	\$	\$

The incompleteness of **BFOA** basic implies that it also fails to be *categorical.* A set of postulates is said to be *categorical* if all of its models are *isomorphic* (Greek *iso:* 'same' and *morphe:* 'form') in the sense that the *same* diagram serves for all of them, apart from the relabelling of nodes.[7] The non-categoricity of basic arithmetic can be seen immediately from the fact that the standard interpretation $\mathfrak{N}$ is not isomorphic to the interpretation $\mathfrak{B}$ defined previously. For no relabelling of nodes can ever convert $\mathfrak{N}$'s diagram (*) into $\mathfrak{B}$'s diagram (**), since the latter contains loops and the former doesn't.

The incompleteness of **BFOA** is a kind of deductive weakness: certain arithmetical sentences that one would expect to be logical consequences of it follow turn out not to be. This weakness can be overcome by adding to it a *second-order* postulate known as the *Principle of Mathematical Induction.* Informally, this is the rule of arithmetic that states:

> *for any property* **P** *of natural numbers, if* 0 *has the property* **P** *and if, for any number x, that* $x+1$ *has the property* **P** *follows from the assumption that x has the property* **P**, *then every number has the property* **P**.

This can be expressed by the second-order sentence

$$\textbf{Ind} \quad \forall P[[P0 \wedge \forall x(Px \rightarrow Psx)] \rightarrow \forall xPx],$$

where P is a predicate variable.

Basic second-order arithmetic (BSOA) is obtained by adding **Ind** to **BFOA.**

We have seen that **BFOA** has models that differ in essential respects from the standard interpretation $\mathfrak{N}$. But its second-order extension **BSOA** does not suffer from this defect. In fact, **BSOA** is categorical; all of its models are

[7] To be precise, an *isomorphism* between two **L**-structures $\mathfrak{A} = (A, \{R_i : j \in I\}, \{g_i : j \in J\}, \{e_k : k \in K\})$ and $\mathfrak{A}' = (A', \{R'_i : j \in I\}, \{g'_i : j \in J\}, \{e'_k : k \in K\})$ is a bijective function $F : A \rightarrow A'$ satisfying, for each $i \in I, j \in J, k \in K$, the conditions $F(e_k) = e'_k$, $F[Ri] = R'I$, for any $a_1, \ldots, a_{m(j)} \in A, g'_j(Fa_1, \ldots, Fa_{m(j)}) = F(g_j(a_1, \ldots, a_{m(j)}))$.

isomorphic to $\mathfrak{N}$. The first, and crucial, step in demonstrating this is to establish what we shall call the 'exhaustion principle'.

Exhaustion principle*. Models of* **Ind** *are exactly those interpretations in which (the interpretations of the terms on) the list 0, s0, ss0, sss0, ... exhausts the whole domain of the interpretation.*

To see this, suppose that $\mathfrak{A}$ is a model of **Ind**. Let $M = \{0^{\mathfrak{A}}, (s0)^{\mathfrak{A}}, (ss0)^{\mathfrak{A}}, \ldots\}$ and let P be a predicate symbol such that $P^{\mathfrak{A}} = M$. (We may assume without loss of generality that such exists by simply adding a new predicate symbol to **L** and interpreting it as *M*.) Then $P0$ and $\forall x(Px \to P_{Sx})$ are both true in $\mathfrak{A}$. Since $\mathfrak{A} \models$ **Ind**, it follows that $\forall xPx$ is true in $\mathfrak{A}$. But the truth of this means precisely that $A = M$.

Conversely, suppose that the domain A of an interpretation $\mathfrak{A}$ coincides with $\{0^{\mathfrak{A}}, (s0)^{\mathfrak{A}}, (ss0)^{\mathfrak{A}}, \ldots\}$. Let **P** be any property defined on A, and let P be a predicate symbol such that $P^{\mathfrak{A}} =$ **P**. (Again, we can always add a new predicate symbol to **L** and interpret it as *U*.) Now assume that $P0$ and $\forall x(Px \to Psx)$ are both true in $\mathfrak{A}$. We claim that $\forall xPx$ is also true in $\mathfrak{A}$. If not, then some element of A fails to satisfy $P^{\mathfrak{A}}$. Since $P0$ is true in $\mathfrak{A}$, this element cannot be $0^{\mathfrak{A}}$ and so is of the form $\left(s^n0\right)^{\mathrm{A}}$ for some $n \geq 1$ (here, s^n0 is 0 preceded by n s's). Let n be the least number such that $\left(s^n0\right)^{\mathfrak{A}}$ fails to satisfy $P^{\mathfrak{A}}$. Then $n \geq 1$ and $Ps^{n-1}0$ is true in $\mathfrak{A}$. Since $\forall x(Px \to Psx)$ is true in $\mathfrak{A}$, it follows that $Ps^{n-1}0 \to \mathrm{Ps}^{\mathrm{n}}0$ is true in $\mathfrak{A}$, and hence, Ps^n0 is true in $\mathfrak{A}$. This contradicts the choice of n, and it follows that $\forall xPx$ must have been true in $\mathfrak{A}$ after all. Accordingly,

$$P0 \wedge \forall x(Px \to Psx) \to \forall xPx$$

is true in $\mathfrak{A}$; since the interpretation of P was an arbitrary property defined on A, we conclude that the **Ind** is true in $\mathfrak{A}$.

Second-order successor arithmetic (**SOSA**) is defined to be the weakened version of **BSOA** whose postulates are **B1**, **B2**, and **Ind.** We show that **SOSA** *is categorical; each of its models being isomorphic to* $\mathfrak{N}$.

To prove this, let $\mathfrak{A}$ be a model of **SOSA**. Then, by the exhaustion principle, the domain of $\mathfrak{A}$ consists of the interpretations of the terms on the list

$$(*) \quad 0,\ s0,\ ss0,\ sss0, \ldots$$

The truth of **B2** in $\mathfrak{A}$ implies that the sentences $0 \neq \mathrm{s}0$, $0 \neq \mathrm{ss}0$, $0 \neq \mathrm{sss}0$ are all true in $\mathfrak{A}$. It now follows from the truth of **B1** in $\mathfrak{A}$ that distinct members of the list (*) receive distinct interpretations in $\mathfrak{A}$. (For if not, then, for example, $sss0 = \mathrm{sssss}0$ would be true in $\mathfrak{A}$, and three applications of **B1** would show $0 = \mathrm{ss}0$ to be true in $\mathfrak{A}$, contradicting what we have already established.) It follows that the diagram of $\mathfrak{A}$ looks like:

$$0^{\mathfrak{A}} \to 1^{\mathfrak{A}} \to 2^{\mathfrak{A}} \to 3^{\mathfrak{A}} \to \ldots .$$

Clearly, this diagram can be relabelled so as to convert it into the diagram of the standard interpretation $\mathfrak{N}$, namely,

$$0 \to \mathbf{1} \to 2 \to 3 \to \ldots .$$

Therefore, $\mathfrak{A}$ and $\mathfrak{N}$ are isomorphic.

By complicating this argument, it can be shown that each model of **BSOA** is isomorphic to $\mathfrak{N}$ so that **BSOA** is also categorical.

The categoricity of **BSOA** means that – unlike **BFOA** – it furnishes a *complete characterization* of the natural number system in the following sense:

> *For any sentence σ in the vocabulary of* **BSOA**, *σ is a logical consequence of* **BSOA** *if and only if σ is true in the standard interpretation* $\mathfrak{N}$.

To prove this, we observe that if σ is a logical consequence of **BSOA**, it must be true in every model of it, and so in particular, it must be true in $\mathfrak{N}$. Conversely, suppose σ is true in $\mathfrak{N}$, and let $\mathfrak{A}$ be any model of **BSOA**. Since **BSOA** is categorical, $\mathfrak{A}$ is isomorphic to $\mathfrak{N}$, so since σ is true in $\mathfrak{N}$, it must also be true in $\mathfrak{A}$. Therefore, σ is a logical consequence of **BSOA.**

We finally note that **Ind** has several non-isomorphic models, which shows that taken *by itself*, it is not categorical. These models are based on the following four diagrams, in which the denotations of *s* and *0* are displayed: as usual, each arrow goes from an element to its 'successor'.

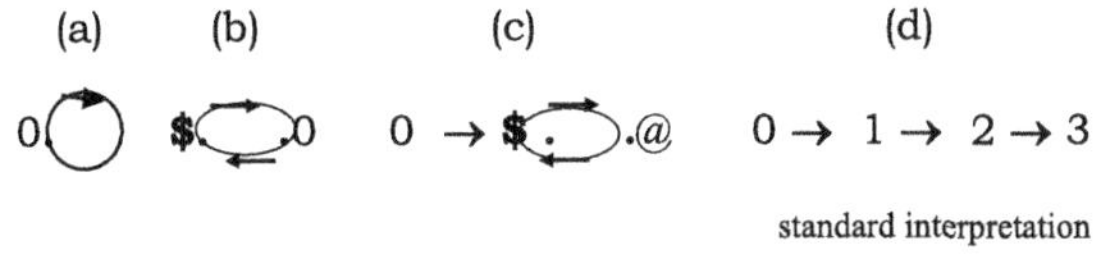

It is evident that no one of these diagrams can be converted into another by relabelling nodes since they all contain different numbers of nodes: 1, 2, 3, ∞, respectively. The interpretations are therefore non-isomorphic.

Note that **B1** is false in interpretation (c), and **B2** is false in both (a) and (b).

1.3 The Limitations of Second-Order Logic

While second-order logic has great expressive power, that very expressive power is the source of certain limitations, which we now describe.

One of the most useful metatheorems of first-order logic is the *compactness theorem.* This states that if each finite subset of a set Σ of first-order sentences has a model, then so does Σ. But the fact that the property of having a finite domain is expressible in second-order logic leads to the failure of the compactness theorem.

This can be seen as follows. For each $n \geq 1$ write σ_n for the first-order sentence

$$\exists v_1 \exists v_2 \ldots \exists v_n (v_1 \neq v_2 \wedge \ldots \wedge v_1 \neq v_n \wedge v_2 \neq v_3 \wedge \ldots \wedge v_2 \neq v_n \wedge \ldots \wedge v_{n-1} \neq v_n)$$

(σ_n says that the domain has at least n elements). Now, let Σ be the set of sentences $\{$ **Fin**, $\sigma_1, \sigma_2, \ldots\}$ where **Fin** is the second-order sentence expressing finitude formulated earlier. Then, clearly, each finite subset of Σ has a model, but Σ itself does not. Accordingly, the compactness theorem fails for second-order logic.

The most important metatheoretical feature of first-order logic is that the *semantic* notion $\models$ of first-order logical consequence can be recast in a purely *syntactic* form. This can be done by furnishing first-order logic[8] with a *derivability apparatus,* thus turning into a *deductive system.* There are various ways of doing this. Here, we describe a method based on the idea of a *formal derivation* or *proof,* resting in its turn on a body of formal *axioms* and *rules of inference.*

The *axioms* and *rules of inference* for classical first-order logic in **L** are specified as follows. As *axioms,* we take all formulas of the form:

(i) $\alpha \rightarrow (\beta \rightarrow \alpha)$

(ii) $[\alpha \rightarrow (\beta \rightarrow \gamma) \rightarrow [(\alpha \rightarrow \beta) \rightarrow (\alpha \rightarrow \gamma)]$

(iii) $\alpha \rightarrow (\beta \rightarrow \alpha \wedge \beta)$

(iv) $\alpha \wedge \beta \rightarrow \alpha \qquad \alpha \wedge \beta \rightarrow \beta$

(v) $\alpha \rightarrow \alpha \vee \beta \qquad \beta \rightarrow \alpha \vee \beta$

(vi) $(\alpha \rightarrow \gamma) \rightarrow [(\beta \rightarrow \gamma) \rightarrow (\alpha \vee \beta \rightarrow \gamma)]$

(vii) $(\alpha \rightarrow \beta) \rightarrow [(\alpha \rightarrow \neg\beta) \rightarrow \neg\alpha]$

(viii) $\neg\alpha \rightarrow (\alpha \rightarrow \beta)$

(ix) $(\alpha \leftrightarrow \beta) \rightarrow [(\alpha \rightarrow \beta) \wedge (\beta \rightarrow \alpha)] \qquad [(\alpha \rightarrow \beta) \wedge (\beta \rightarrow \alpha)] \rightarrow (\alpha \leftrightarrow \beta)$

(x) $\neg\neg\alpha \rightarrow \alpha$

(xi) $\alpha(t) \rightarrow \exists x\alpha(x)$ $\forall x\alpha(x) \rightarrow \alpha(t)$ (x free in α and t free for x in α[9])

(xii) $x = x$

(xiii) $\alpha(x) \wedge x = y \rightarrow \alpha(y)$

As *rules of inference,* we take

Modus ponens $\dfrac{\alpha,\ \alpha \rightarrow \beta}{\beta}$,

Quantifier Rules $\dfrac{\beta \rightarrow \alpha(x)}{\beta \rightarrow \forall x\alpha(x)} \qquad \dfrac{\alpha(x) \rightarrow \beta}{\exists x\alpha(x) \rightarrow \beta}$ (x not free in β).

[8] We emphasize that here we are concerned with *classical* logic. In Section 3, *intuitionistic* logic will enter the picture.

[9] A term t is said to be *free for* x in a formula α if no variable occurring in t becomes bound when t is substituted for x in α.

A *derivation,* or *proof,* in **L** of φ from a set Σ of sentences of **L** is a finite sequence $\psi_1, \ldots, \psi_n$ of **L**-formulas, with $\psi_n = \varphi$, each member of which either is an axiom, a member of Σ, or else follows from previous ψ_i by applying one of the rules of inference. We say that φ is *derivable*, or *provable, from* Σ, and write

$$\Sigma \vdash \varphi,$$

if there is a derivation of φ from Σ. Σ is said to be *consistent* if for no **L**-formula φ do we have $\Sigma \vdash \varphi \wedge \neg\varphi$. If $\varnothing \vdash \varphi$, we write $\vdash \varphi$ and call φ a *theorem* of **L.** We call $\vdash$ the *derivability relation* of first-order logic.

The key feature of the relation $\vdash$ is that it can be shown to be *equivalent* to the relation $\models$. This is the *completeness theorem* for first-order logic. In particular, it follows that *the logically valid sentences of first-order logic coincide with its theorems.* This is the *completeness property* of first-order logic.

The various sorts of derivability apparatus for first-order logic have in common the feature that they all lead to the completeness theorem so that the body of theorems T does not vary. Moreover, whatever sort of derivability apparatus is used, in each case, T can be shown to be *effectively enumerable.* This means that if we are given a means of listing, or enumerating, the symbols constituting the first-order vocabulary, leading in its turn to an enumeration of the formulas of first-order logic, then the derivability apparatus can be used to distil from the latter enumeration, in an effective, calculable way, an enumeration of the members of T. Let us sum this up by saying that derivability in first-order logic is *effective.*

Can second-order logic be furnished with a derivability apparatus which is both complete and shows it to be effective in the analogous sense? As we shall see, the categoricity of **BSOA**, established earlier, together with the basic theorem of Tarski on the undefinability of truth,[10] shows that the answer is no.

To be precise, we shall use the following consequence[11] of Tarski's theorem:

(**T**) *There is no effective enumeration of the set of (first- or second-order) sentences of arithmetic, which are* true *in the standard interpretation* $\mathfrak{N}$ *of arithmetic.*

We show that the assumption that a complete and effective derivability apparatus for second-order logic exists contradicts (**T**).

Thus, suppose that a complete and effective derivability apparatus, **D**, say, for second-order logic exists, and write $\vdash$ for its derivability relation. Let β be the conjunction of the postulates of **BSOA**. Then for any (first- or second-order) sentence σ of the vocabulary of arithmetic, we would have

[10] For an account of Tarski's theorem, see, for example, Bell and Machover (1977), chapter 7.

[11] Bell and Machover (1977), chapter 7, corollary 5.5.

(*) $\mathfrak{N} \vDash \sigma \Leftrightarrow\ \vdash \beta \rightarrow \sigma.$

From the effectiveness of **D**, it follows that there is an effective enumeration of the sentences σ for which $\vdash \beta \rightarrow \sigma$, and we deduce from (*) that there must also be an effective enumeration of the sentences true in $\mathfrak{N}$. This contradicts (**T**), and we conclude that no complete and effective derivability apparatus for second-order logic can exist.

This fact indicates that the meaning of the second-order quantifiers 'for all relations' or 'for all subsets' cannot be completely captured in a formal way. However, the natural extension of the first-order deductive apparatus to second-order logic, described later, continues to be effective and, it turns out, complete for interpretations in which the *second-order quantifiers are construed in a suitably restricted sense.* This can be motivated by considering the second-order sentence **Fin** expressing finiteness, which was introduced earlier.

This sentence **Fin** is *false* under any second-order interpretation with an infinite domain. This is because the quantifier '∀X' is interpreted as 'for *any* binary relation *X*'. But if we were to change the interpretation of '∀*X*' to 'for any binary relation which is the graph of the identity function or a constant function', then **Fin** would come out *true.*

This raises the possibility of weakening the interpretation of the second-order quantifier '∀*X*' to 'for all *prescribed* relations (or subsets)', where 'prescribed' means 'being a member of a collection of relations defined on (or subsets of) the domain *specified in advance*'. This leads to *Henkin semantics*[12] for second-order logic, named after the American logician Leon Henkin. This is based on the idea of a *Henkin interpretation* of second-order logic. In a Henkin interpretation, a structure $\mathfrak{A}$, known as a *Henkin structure,* now has to be furnished, for each $n \geq 1$, with a specified collection $\boldsymbol{C}_n$ of *n*-ary relations defined on the domain *A*. Then clauses 10 and 11 above for interpreting the second-order quantifiers become

10') $\mathfrak{A} \vDash_{\boldsymbol{R}} \exists\ V_m^{(n)} \varphi \Leftrightarrow$ for some n-ary relation $Q \in C_n$, $\mathfrak{A} \vDash_{[m|Q]\boldsymbol{R}} \varphi$,

11') $\mathfrak{A} \vDash_{\boldsymbol{R}} \exists\ V_m^{(n)} \varphi \Leftrightarrow$ for any n-ary relation $Q \in C_n$, $\mathfrak{A} \vDash_{[m|Q]\boldsymbol{R}} \varphi$.

A *full* Henkin interpretation is one in which each C_n is the full power set of A^n. Clearly, by restricting Henkin interpretations to full interpretations, we obtain the original semantics – call it the *standard semantics* – for second-order logic.

Now the proof that **BSOA** is categorical under standard semantics employed the exhaustion lemma. But if we examine the proof of the latter, we find that it is

[12] Henkin (1950).

not valid under the Henkin interpretation. From the truth of $P0, \forall x(Px \rightarrow Psx)$ and **Ind** in a Henkin interpretation, it does not necessarily follow that $\forall xPx$ is also true there because the denotation of P may not be among the prescribed predicates of the interpretation. Accordingly, we cannot conclude that **BSOA** is categorical under the Henkin interpretation. The reason for this is that the Henkin interpretation embraces more structures than does the standard one so that categoricity under the Henkin interpretation is a stronger notion than its standard counterpart.

Since **BSOA** is not categorical under the Henkin interpretation, we cannot go on, as we did previously, to invoke Tarski's theorem to infer that there is no complete and effective deductive apparatus for second-order logic *under the Henkin interpretation.* And, in fact, it can be shown that a straightforward, natural extension of the first-order logical apparatus to second-order logic is effective and complete under the Henkin interpretation.

This extension to second-order logic of the first-order logical apparatus is obtained by adding to the latter as axioms all formulas of the form

$$\forall X\varphi(X) \rightarrow \varphi^* \qquad \varphi^* \rightarrow \exists X\varphi(X),$$

where $\varphi(X)$ is a formula with a free n-ary relation variable X and φ^* is the result of replacing each occurrence of $X(t_1, \ldots, t_n)$ in φ by $\psi(t_1, \ldots, t_n)$, where ψ is a formula such that no free variables among the t_I become bound after the replacement.

As additional rules of inference, we take

$$\frac{\varphi \rightarrow \psi(X)}{\varphi \rightarrow \forall X\varphi(X)} \qquad\qquad \frac{\Psi(X) \rightarrow \varphi}{\exists X\psi(X) \rightarrow \varphi},$$

where X is not free in φ.

With these additional axioms and rules of inference, the resulting deductive system for second-order logic is effective and complete under the Henkin interpretation. The argument is essentially the same as for first-order logic. In essence, the completeness of this deductive system for second-order logic results from the fact that Henkin semantics is essentially the first-order semantics of the many-sorted first-order logic associated with second-order logic.

1.4 Higher-Order Logic Based on Types

It is clear that the step by which we moved from a first-order to a second-order vocabulary, namely, by introducing second-level variables and subjecting them to (second-level) quantification, can be repeated. Thus, we can ascend to a third-order vocabulary, by introducing third-level variables and constants (these will include, e.g., variables and constants ranging over properties of properties and relations between relations) and suitably enlarging the class of formulas to include as atomic formulas any third-level n-ary term followed by n second-level terms (i.e., second-level variables or constants), as well as allowing quantification over third-level variables. This ascent can be continued indefinitely, leading to a hierarchy of types of terms, with terms and quantifiers of every (finite) level. It is to be noted that the hierarchy of types so generated will be *strict*, in the sense that entities of one level can take as arguments only items of the *next lower level,* and all other ways of putting symbols together will be deemed meaningless. This requirement was the basis for Russell's first attempt at formulating a type theory designed to avoid the set-theoretic antinomies (see Section 2), but it seems in general too restrictive, since the variables and constants of a given level then correspond just to homogeneous relations of entities of the *next lower* level. While it is natural enough that an entity of a given level should represent relations of entities of a lower level, there is no compelling reason to put any further restriction on the levels of these latter entities, so long as each of them *is* of a lower level than that of the given entity. In other words, it seems natural to extend relation variables to *mixed-level* relations. This leads to the idea of a (general) *higher-order vocabulary.*

Higher-order vocabularies are built on a generalization of the concept of level called a *type.* Types are objects that are constructed in a finite number of steps, starting with an arbitrarily chosen object ★, according to the following rules:

- ★ is a type called the *initial type.*
- If $\tau_1, \ldots, \tau_n$ are types, then the sequence $(\tau_1, \ldots, \tau_n)$ is a type.

Now, in addition to the usual logical operators, quantifiers, and so on, a higher-order vocabulary is equipped, for each type τ, with variables and constants – *terms* – of type τ. Variables and constants of type ★ are identified with individual variables and constants. Thus, for each non-initial type τ, the higher-order vocabulary will contain a list $X^{(\tau)}, Y^{(\tau)}, Z^{(\tau)}, \ldots$ of variables of type τ and a list $P^{(\tau)}, Q^{(\tau)}, Z^{(\tau)}$ of constants of type τ. Atomic formulas are defined to be: (i) all expressions of the form $s = t$, where s and t are terms of the same type and (ii) all expressions of the form $X^{(\tau)}(t_1, \ldots, t_n)$ or $P^{(\tau)}(t_1, \ldots, t_n)$, where $\tau = (\tau_1, \ldots, \tau_n)$ is a non-initial type and $t_1, \ldots, t_n$ are terms of types $\tau_1, \ldots, \tau_n$.[13] Non-atonic formulas are defined as before.

Higher-order vocabularies provide the scaffolding for *higher-order logic.* The *derivability apparatus* for higher-order logic can be set up in a way similar

[13] Notice that this definition of atomic formula makes the assignment of different multiplicities to terms unnecessary. Multiplicity has, in effect, been absorbed into the types themselves.

to that for second-order logic. The *semantics* of higher-order logic can be formulated by introducing the concept of *higher-order Henkin structure*, the natural extension to higher orders of the notion of previously formulated Henkin structure. The notion of an *interpretation* of a higher-order vocabulary in a higher-order Henkin structure can then be introduced in a way similar to that of an interpretation of a second-order vocabulary in a Henkin structure. The various results we have established for second-order logic can then, suitably formulated, be extended to higher-order logic.

Because of the underlying presence of a type framework in its formulation, higher-order logic can be regarded as a version of *type theory,* a topic to which we now turn.

2 Type Theory and Its Origins

2.1 The Origins of Type Theory

The roots of type theory lie in set theory, to be precise, in Bertrand Russell's efforts to resolve the paradoxes besetting set theory at the end of the nineteenth century. In analyzing these paradoxes, Russell had come to find the set, or class, concept itself philosophically perplexing, even dubious, and the theory of types can be seen as the outcome of his struggle to resolve these perplexities. But, at first, he seems to have regarded type theory as little more than a faute de mieux.

In June 1901, Russell learned of the set-theoretic paradox, known to Cantor by 1899, that issued from applying the latter's theorem concerning power sets to the class V of all sets. According to that theorem, the class of all subclasses of V would, impossibly, have to possess a cardinality exceeding that of V. This stimulated Russell to formulate the paradox that came to bear his name (although it was independently formulated by Zermelo at about the same time) concerning the class of all classes, not members of themselves (or predicates, not predicable of themselves). If we write R for the class of all classes, not members of themselves, Russell's paradox is the assertion that R is a member of itself if and only if it is not.

Grasping that his paradox applied also to the logical system previously elaborated by Frege in his *Grundgesetze*, Russell communicated it to Frege in June 1902, thereby occasioning, in the latter's own words, the 'greatest surprise, and I would almost say, consternation, since it has shaken the basis on which I intended to build arithmetic'. Frege responded by attempting to patch up the postulate of his system (Basic Law V) subject to the paradox, fashioning a repair that Russell was initially inclined to endorse (see the final note to Appendix A of

The Principles of Mathematics).[14] Frege's repair, in fact, proved inadequate, but in any case, Russell had already begun to search for a solution to the paradox as it applied to classes. This led him to propose the theory, or doctrine, of types.

It is of interest to see how Russell's doctrine of types emerges from his analysis of classes in the *Principles*. He puts forward the following definition of a class:

> *A class is an object uniquely determined by a propositional function,*[15] *and determined equally by any equivalent propositional function.*

Here, Russell is, in essence, adopting an *extensional*[16] view of classes.[17]

He then considers the following possible characterizations of the class notion:

> *A class may be identified with (α) the predicate, (β) the class concept, (γ) the concept of the class, (δ) Frege's range, (ε) the numerical conjunction of the terms of the class, (ζ) the whole composed of the terms of the class.*

To understand what Russell intends by the first three of these, let us consider the term *person*. Here, (α) then corresponds to the predicate … *is human*, (β) to the function of *person* in propositions such as *is a person,* and (γ) to the concept of the *class of persons*. Clearly, each of these characterizations is intensional in nature, in that the identity of the object in question depends in an essential way on the term *person* and not on anything equivalent to it (e.g., 'rational featherless biped'). Accordingly, none of these can be taken as a satisfactory determination of the notion of the essentially extensional notion of class.

Under head (δ), 'Frege's range' refers to the device introduced by Frege in the *Grundgesetze* by which each function is assigned an object called its *range* in

---

14 Russell (1903).

15 Here is the usual definition (Lewis 1918): A *proposition* is any expression that is either true or false; a *propositional function* is an expression, containing one or more variables, that becomes a proposition when each of the variables is replaced by one of its values from a domain of individuals.

16 The term *extensional* is to be contrasted with the term *intensional*. Typically, the intension of a concept is given by its meaning and its extension by the collection of things embodying the concept. Two concepts may have entirely different intensions and yet have identical extensions. For example, the two concepts 'square number' and 'sum of a sequence of successive odd numbers starting with 1' have different intensions but identical extensions.

17 But interestingly, Russell earlier remarks that he was led to an extensional view of classes 'against [his] inclination' and only because of 'the necessity of discovering some entity determinate for a given propositional function, and the same for any equivalent propositional function'. This would seem to be essentially the same reason Frege was led to introduce ranges or, more pertinently, their special case extensions of concepts. Russell goes on to say that the only entities he has been able to discover that meet the requirements are, first, the class as one of all objects making the given propositional function true and, second, the class (also as one) of all propositional functions equivalent to the given function. One notes that the first expedient involves a type reduction and the second a type augmentation.

such a way that two functions are assigned the same range precisely when they have identical values for all values of their arguments. This is Basic Law V, which Russell had already shown to be inconsistent. In view of this, Russell is led to observe that '(δ) suffers from a doubt as to their being such an entity, and also from the fact that, if ranges are terms, the contradiction is inevitable'. This determination is equally unsatisfactory.

Under (ε), we have the *class-as-many,* or *plurality*. Russell regards this notion as 'logically unobjectionable' since he thinks that the existence of classes-as-many is guaranteed ontologically, and so, at the very least, classes-as-many can always be assumed to exist without falling into contradiction. But classes-as-many suffer from the drawback that they are not single entities, except when the class has only one member.

Finally, category (ζ) is the *class-as-one.*[18] The problem here is that Russell's paradox shows that classes-as-one do not always exist.

Russell is accordingly left with no satisfactory way of defining classes. Yet, as he says, 'without a single object to represent an extension, Mathematics crumbles'. In the end, he is forced to adopt (ε), the class-as-many, as the definition of a class. This requires abandoning the doctrine that the subject of a proposition is always a single term; instead, it can be essentially many terms. Once this is accepted, one sees that the plural nature of classes does not prevent them from being 'counted as though each were a genuine unity'. But in that case, Russell observes that it then becomes necessary 'to distinguish (1) terms, (2) classes, (3) classes of classes, and so on *ad infinitum*'. Moreover, these collections will be disjoint, and to be able to assert $x \in u$ requires that the collection to which x belongs should be of a level one lower than that to which u belongs. This expedient leads to a resolution of the paradox, since $x \in x$ has now been rendered a meaningless proposition. The hierarchy of collections (1), (2), (3), … is the germ of the doctrine of types.

In Appendix B to the *Principles*, entitled *The Doctrine of Types*, Russell states that he is putting forward the doctrine 'tentatively, as affording a possible solution of the contradiction', but it 'requires, in all probability, to be transformed into some subtler shape before it can answer all difficulties'. He proceeds to explain exactly what he means by a type:

> *Every propositional function φ(x) … has, in addition to its range of truth, a range of significance,* that is, *a range within which x must lie if φ(x) is to be a proposition at all, whether true or false. This is the first point in the theory of*

[18] The difference between a class-as-many and a class-as-one can be illustrated by a simple example. Consider the term 'the United States Senate'. Regarded as a collection of 100 different senators, the term denotes a class-as-many. Regarded as the statutory body defined in the US constitution, the term denotes a class-as-one.

> *types; the second point is that ranges of significance form* types, that is, *if x belongs to the range of significance of $\varphi(x)$, then there is a class of objects, the* type *of x, all of which must also belong to the range of significance of $\varphi(x)$; however, φ may be varied; and the range of significance is always either a single type or a sum of several whole types.*

As observed previously, Russell believed the doctrine of types to be adequate for resolving the paradox for classes. But according to his definition of type, propositions *themselves* can serve as the constituting objects for types. Russell proceeds to formulate a paradox for propositions similar to that for classes, which he does not think is resolved by the doctrine of types as he has formulated it. This paradox may be stated in the following way. For any class P of propositions, write $\sqcap P$ for the proposition *every proposition in P is true.* Russell makes the key (but as we shall see later, questionable) assumption that for classes P, Q of propositions,

$$(*) \quad P \neq Q \Rightarrow \sqcap P \neq \sqcap Q,$$

or equivalently

$$(**) \quad \sqcap P = \sqcap Q \Rightarrow P = Q.$$

Now let Q be the class of propositions p for which there is a class P of propositions such that $p = \sqcap P$ and $p \notin P$. If one now writes q for $\sqcap Q$, then, using $(*)$, $q \in Q \Leftrightarrow q \notin Q$. Faced with this conclusion, Russell remarks:

> *It is possible of course to hold that propositions themselves are of various types and that their logical products must have propositions of only one type as factors. But this suggestion seems harsh and highly artificial.*

A number of years were to pass before Russell came finally to adopt this 'harsh and highly artificial' suggestion in the form of the ramified theory of types.

Russell remarks that if the identity relation is replaced by the relation of *logical equivalence,* then there is no reason to uphold implication (*), and the contradiction disappears. But this escape is blocked, according to Russell, because

> *it is quite self-evident that equivalent propositional functions are often not identical.*

At this point, then, Russell could see no way out of the contradiction.

Some light can be shed on this matter by the following observations. In deriving the contradiction, it is (*) (or (**)) that is the culprit. Writing **Prop** for the class of all propositions, each asserts that the function $P \mapsto \sqcap P$ is one-one from the class of subclasses of **Prop** to **Prop.** And this, as is now well known (and likely also then to

Russell himself), violates Cantor's theorem. In Boolos (1997), it is shown how to prove Cantor's theorem through the provision of explicit counterexamples.[19] His argument can be adapted to produce a *counterexample* to (**). By Boolos's argument, there exists a subclass M of **Prop** and a well-ordering $\prec$ of M such that (1) $\sqcap M \in M$ and (2) for $p \in M$, $p = \sqcap\{q \in \mathbf{Prop}: q \prec p\}$.[20] Now let $N = \{q : q \prec \sqcap M\}$. Then $\sqcap M \notin N$, and so it follows from (1) that $M \neq N$. But, by (1) and (2), $\sqcap M = \sqcap N$. The classes of propositions M and N thus together constitute a counterexample to (**).

It is tempting to speculate that, had Russell known of this argument, he might have been led to abandon (*) and so perhaps have been more inclined to accept the adequacy of his early theory of types.

2.2 Russell's Ramified Theory of Types

It had also become apparent to Russell that his initial theory of types was incapable of resolving certain other logical paradoxes that had arisen in the foundations of mathematics, for example, the *Liar Paradox*[21] and the *Heterological Paradox.*[22] He attempted to meet the challenge in a number of different ways. But he soon became aware of the inadequacies of these approaches and returned once again to the theory of types. The refined theory of types that resulted from his labours was first outlined in a paper published in 1908: 'Mathematical Logic as Based on the Theory of Types'.[23] Russell prefaces his paper by remarking that while the theory he is about to present 'recommends itself … in the first instance, by the ability to solve certain contradictions', it 'seems not wholly dependent on this indirect recommendation'. It has also 'a certain consonance with common sense which makes it inherently credible'. It is the theory's latter feature that, in part, led Russell to put it forward as a foundation for mathematical logic – and so also for mathematics.

Russell offers an account of the various contradictions with which he is concerned, finding that they all have in common 'the assumption of a totality such that, if it were legitimate, it would at once be enlarged by new members

[19] Boolos's argument is itself an adaptation of the first argument Zermelo used to derive the well-ordering theorem from the Axiom of Choice.

[20] If we express the assertion $q \prec p$ by saying that q is *below p,* then (2) may be expressed as: for any proposition $p \in M$, p is identical with the proposition *every proposition below p is true.*

[21] The Liar Paradox arises when one makes the assertion *the statement I am now making is false.* Clearly, this assertion is true if and only if it is false.

[22] The Heterological Paradox arises when we define an adjective to be *heterological* if and only if it does not apply to itself (thus, e.g., the adjective 'French' is heterological). It then follows that 'heterological' is heterological if and only if it is not heterological.

[23] Russell (1908).

defined in terms of itself'. This leads to the enunciation of the rule that he calls the *vicious circle principle*, to wit:

> *Whatever involves* all *of a collection must not be one of a collection, or, conversely: If provided a certain collection had a total, it would have members only definable in terms of that total, then the said collection has no total.*

Russell recognized that this principle, being purely negative, 'suffices to show that many theories are wrong, but it does not show how the errors are to be rectified'. Russell saw a positive theory emerging from an analysis of the use of the term 'all' and in particular from drawing a careful distinction between it and the term 'any'. While restrictions must, on pain of contradiction, be imposed on the use of 'all', no such restrictions need be placed on 'any'. Thus, 'all' corresponds to the bound variable of universal quantification, which ranges over a type – the *type* of that variable – while 'any' corresponds to a free variable for which the name of anything can be substituted, irrespective of type.

Russell now proceeds to introduce a theory of types for propositions – an expedient that, we recall, he had shunned in 1903 as being 'harsh and artificial'. The entities populating Russell's typed logical universe are of three kinds: *individuals, propositions,* and *(propositional) functions.* He defines a *type* as 'the range of significance of a propositional function, that is, as the collection of arguments for which the said function has values'. Individuals are decreed to occupy the first, or lowest, type. Types are assigned to propositions through the device of *orders.* Thus, first-order propositions are those whose quantified variables (if any) are individuals: these form the second type. Second-order propositions or functions are then those whose quantified variables are of at most second type and so on.

From the hierarchy of propositions, Russell derives a hierarchy of propositional functions. Now, the hierarchy of propositions may be considered one-dimensional in that just a single number is required to specify its position in the hierarchy. The hierarchy of propositional functions, however, is multidimensional since the type of a propositional function involves not just its order as a proposition but also the orders of its arguments, or free variables. It is this feature of Russell's theory that led to its being called the *ramified* theory of types.

As Quine[24] has pointed out, the logical universe presented by Russell has a number of ambiguous features. For instance, in Russell's formulation, individuals are objects, but propositions and propositional functions are notations,

[24] In his commentary on Russell's paper in Van Heijenoort (1967).

dependent on the vicissitudes of presentation. That being the case, it is far from clear whether Russell is 'assigning types to his objects or to his notations'.

Russell next addresses the question of whether his theory is adequate for the development of mathematics. He gives examples from elementary mathematics to show that the answer is no unless some method is found 'of reducing the order of a propositional function without affecting the truth or falsehood of its values'. To achieve this, he introduces the *Axiom of Reducibility,* which asserts that every propositional function is coextensive – that is, has the same values for the same values of the arguments – with a predicative function (in the same arguments). Hereby, a *predicative* function is meant one in which the types of quantified variables do not exceed the types of the arguments.[25] Russell justifies this postulate on the grounds that it has all the useful consequences flowing from the class concept, without having to go so far as to admit the actual presence of classes.

As Quine[26] observes, this expedient is 'oddly devious'. If every propositional function is coextensive with a predicative one, then attention could have been confined to these latter from the start. In other words, the 'ramification' of types is rendered superfluous; the types of propositional functions could have been made dependent solely on their arguments. Indeed, 'The axiom of reducibility is self-effacing: if it is true, the ramification it was meant to cope with was pointless to begin with'.[27]

Russell's ramified types faced numerous objections of this sort; these will be discussed later.

2.3 Russell's Types versus Zermelo's Sets

In the same year (1908) that Russell published his paper on logical types, Ernst Zermelo published his paper 'Investigations in the Foundations of Set Theory I'.[28] In it, he presents the first axiomatization of set theory. While both Russell and Zermelo's theories were intended to furnish a foundation for mathematics – a framework, that is, within which the usual development of mathematics could proceed free of contradiction – there are a number of differences between the

25 The concept of predicative function is closely tied to the idea of predicative and impredicative definitions. A definition is said to be *impredicative* if it involves a generalization over a totality to which the entity being defined belongs. (An example of an impredicative definition is: a person is *presidential* if and only if, for every property P that all outstanding presidents have, that person also has P. This definition is impredicative because the property of being presidential involves a generalization over the totality of all properties, which includes the property of being presidential itself.) Otherwise, the definition is said to be *predicative*. Impredicative definitions, while not in themselves inconsistent, have been regarded as having a circular character, since the properties or entities they define seem to have to be given in advance.

26 In his commentary on Russell's paper in Van Heijenoort (1967). 27 Ibid.

28 Zermelo (1908).

two approaches. Russell had always maintained that mathematics is, at bottom, logic, and his system naturally reflects that conviction. For Russell, once the correct logical framework has been found, mathematics would then follow, hence his concern with the logical paradoxes and his consequent elaboration of the theory of types as a strategy for circumventing them. Once this had been taken care of, the development of mathematics could proceed along the lines mapped out by the great nineteenth-century German analysts Weierstrass, Dedekind, and Cantor, whose work had so impressed Russell.

In formulating his axiom system for set theory, Zermelo was animated by rather different concerns. In 1904, he published his proof of the *well-ordering theorem* that every set could be well-ordered. The proof excited considerable controversy because of its use of the Axiom of Choice[29] and the vagueness of the set-theoretic background. This led Zermelo to publish a new, improved proof (again based on the Axiom of Choice but in a new formulation) of the well-ordering theorem in 1908, which was itself to be underpinned by the sharpened, axiomatized notion of the set presented in *Investigations.* While designed to avoid the set-theoretic paradoxes, the primary purpose of Zermelo's system was to provide the working mathematician with a reliable foundational toolkit.

While Russell sets or classes were essentially logical objects, Zermelo treated them as mathematical objects subject to certain axiomatic conditions. The most interesting of these latter is the third, the *Axiom of Separation.* This axiom is the counterpart, for sets considered as mathematical objects, of the principle governing their (more precisely, classes) introduction as logical objects, namely, as extensions of propositional functions. Zermelo formulates his axiom by introducing the notion of *definite property* and then stipulating that a definite property separates a subset from a previously given set. Sadly, Zermelo's notion of definite property is itself far from being definite, since in its formulation Zermelo, invokes 'the universally valid laws of logic' but neglects to specify what these are. This shortcoming was later rectified, in various ways, by Weyl, Fraenkel, Skolem, and von Neumann. Zermelo's system, as modified and extended by the latter three as well as Gödel and Bernays, in due course, became the standard foundation of mathematics, a role it still plays today.

Type theory has, by contrast, undergone a more tortuous development and has met with a more complex reception. Its initial phase culminated in Russell and Whitehead's monumental trilogy *Principia Mathematica*[30] of 1910–1913.

[29] There are numerous equivalent formulations of the Axiom of Choice: for example, given any family **F** of disjoint non-empty sets, there exists a set containing exactly one member of each set in **F**. Another is the following 'functional' version: for any binary relation R between sets A and B such that for any $a \in A$ there is $b \in B$ such that Rab, there is a function $f: A \to B$ such that $Raf(a)$ for all $a \in A$.

This is a fully elaborated treatment of the framework introduced by Russell in his 1908 paper. It includes both an Axiom of Infinity[31] and an Axiom of Reducibility.

Classes play a very minor role in *Principia*. By the time *Principia* was written, Russell had come to regard classes as dubious logical entities and so sought to avoid having to postulate their existence outright. Russell and Whitehead see the introduction of classes as arising from the necessity to deal with *extensions*:

> *It is an old dispute whether formal logic should concern itself mainly with intensions or with extensions. In general, logicians whose training was mainly philosophical have decided for intensions, while those whose training was mainly mathematical have decided for extensions. The facts seem to be that, while mathematical logic requires extensions, philosophical logic refuses to supply anything except intensions. Our theory of classes recognizes and reconciles these two apparently opposite facts, by showing that an extension (which is the same as a class) is an incomplete symbol, whose use always acquires its meaning through a reference to an intension.*

In order to be able to handle extensions and yet at the same time avoid any awkward ontological commitments, in *Principia*, classes are introduced, then, as *incomplete symbols*, that is, symbols whose '*uses* are defined, but [which] themselves are not assumed to mean anything at all'. Thus, 'classes … are merely symbolic or linguistic conveniences, not genuine objects as their members are if they are individuals'. In other words, classes are mere shadows.

The reconditeness[32] of *Principia* and its focus on philosophical niceties remote from the concerns of working mathematicians hardly commended it as a practical foundation for their subject. Zermelo's axiomatic approach to sets, by contrast, seemed simpler and closer to the actual practice of mathematics.

Nevertheless, the straightforward, unramified concept of type that Russell had initially considered – in its later evolved form as the basis of *simple type theory*[33] – did come to exert a considerable inference on mathematical logic. And the ramified types of *Principia* also played an important, if largely unremarked role in the development of set theory. In the 1930s, Gödel discovered

---

[31] That is, an axiom asserting the existence of an infinite set.

[32] In this connection, it is worth quoting the following extract from a review of *Principia* in a 1911 number of the London magazine *The Spectator:*

> *It is easy to picture the dismay of the innocent person who out of curiosity looks into the later part of the book. He would come upon whole pages without a single word of English below the headline; he would see, instead, scattered in wild profusion, disconnected Greek and Roman letters of every size interspersed with brackets and dots and inverted commas, with arrows and exclamation marks standing on their heads, and with even more fantastic signs for which he would with difficulty so much as find names.*

[33] See Sections 2.4 and 2.5.

that if the ramification of properties over the natural numbers is extended into the transfinite, the process breaks down at level ω_1, the first uncountable ordinal. (This may be considered a provable form of the Axiom of Reducibility.) This led Gödel to introduce the hierarchy of constructible sets that he employed to prove the relative consistency of the continuum hypothesis and the Axiom of Choice.

Now let us briefly consider the question: what is the essential difference between a type and a set? First thought is that types resemble the syntactic or grammatical categories forming the basis of language in that the specification of types furnishes the conditions for expressions to be well-formed, or meaningful. Everyone knows (instinctively at least) that the linguistic phrase '___*sees*___' becomes grammatical only when the first blank is filled in with a noun or a noun phrase and the second with a noun, a noun phrase, or an adverb.

The typing concept also arises in concrete situations. Consider, for example, an automotive toolkit. Here, one is provided with nuts, bolts, and wrench bits to attach nuts to bolts. This gives three types: **N**, **B**, and **S**. Then given the instruction *Use* ___ *to attach* ___ *to* ___, it is implicit that the blanks are filled in with (names of) components of types **S**, **N**, and **B**, respectively.

This case points up nicely the difference between types and sets. For example, we can consider the concrete *set* or *collection* of, say, nuts, of a given toolkit. If (as is so often the case) a few of these go missing, the *set* of nuts is changed but not the associated *type*. The set, that is, the concrete embodiment of the type, is subject to variation, but the type is not. In a nutshell, sets are extensional; types are intensional.

Here is another illustration. We can take two toolkits and *amalgamate* them. Now, while it would be possible to do this simply by jumbling their contents together – that is, to take their set-theoretical union – in order for the result to remain a toolkit in the specified sense, *typing must be respected*: the nuts, bolts, and wrench bits of each toolkit must be conjoined only with the nuts, bolts, and wrench bits, respectively, of the other.

Sets and types, while different, are nevertheless clearly related. Indeed, since each type gives rise to the set of entities of that type, a set may be regarded as a *type considered in extension*. Clearly, different types can give rise to the same set: for example, those old chestnuts the types 'rational featherless biped' and 'human being' are distinct, but their associated sets are (terrestrially, at least) identical. Again, types are intensional, while sets are extensional.

Now sets may also be regarded as *properties* considered in extension. This, conjoined with the fact that sets may be regarded as types considered in extension, might suggest that types are just properties. But that would be a mistake. While the domain of properties is closed under the usual logical operations, these operations are not (in general) defined for types at all. For example, we may consider 'natural number' and 'circle' as types, but we do not similarly admit 'natural number or circle' as a type.

The realm of types is, in fact, now customarily taken to be closed not under logical operations but under what are in fact *mathematical* operations. These may include the Cartesian product ×, the exponential or function type operation →, and the power type operation **P**. Here, for types **A, B**, $\mathbf{A} \times \mathbf{B}$ is the common type of pairs (*a, b*) with *a* of type **A** and *b* of type **B**; **PA** is the type of sets of entities of type **A**; and $\mathbf{A} \to \mathbf{B}$ is the type of correspondences (functions) between entities of types **A, B**, respectively.

The idea that a set may be regarded as a type considered in extension suggests a way of representing (simple) type theory in set theory, namely, just interpret types as sets and function types $\mathbf{A} \to \mathbf{B}$ as the set of functions from (the set corresponding to) **A** to (the set corresponding to) **B**. The representation of set theory within type theory is an altogether subtler affair. The problem here is to represent within type theory the membership relation, which is defined for all pairs of sets. This has been achieved in an elegant manner by Miquel (2001) using the notions of pointed graph and bisimilarity. The idea is to interpret sets as pointed graphs and then to observe that pointed graphs can be represented as types.

A *pointed graph* is a triple $\mathbf{A} = (A, R, a)$ with A, a set; R, a binary relation on A; and $a \in A$. A *bisimilarity* between two pointed graphs $\mathbf{A} = (A, R, a)$ and $\mathbf{B} = (B, S, b)$ is a relation $\approx$ between A and B satisfying the conditions:

- $\forall x \in A \ \forall X' \in A \ \forall y \in B[x'Rx \wedge x \approx y \Rightarrow \exists y' \in B(y'Sy \wedge x' \approx y']$
- $\forall y \in B \ \forall y' \in B \ \forall x \in A[y'Sy \wedge x \approx y \Rightarrow \exists x' \in A(x'Rx \wedge x' \approx y)]$
- $a \approx b$

Two pointed graphs **A** and **B** are *bisimilar,* written $\mathbf{A} \sim \mathbf{B}$, if there is a bisimilarity between them. It is readily checked that bisimilarity is an equivalence relation.

We shall require the *transitive closure* τ (*A*) of set *A*: this is the set whose elements are *A* itself, the members of *A*, the members of members of *A*, and so on. Now, let $\mathbf{A}^*$ be the pointed graph (τ (*A*), $\in$ $|\tau$ (*A*), *A*). It can then be shown that for any sets[34] *A* and *B*,

$$\mathbf{A}* \sim \mathbf{B}* \Leftrightarrow A = B$$

It follows that

$$(*) \quad A \in B \Leftrightarrow \exists X(X \in B \wedge \mathbf{X}* \sim \mathbf{A}*).$$

[34] That is, *well-founded* sets, sets satisfying the Axiom of Foundation.

This last equivalence, which expresses set membership in terms of bisimilarity of pointed graphs – called *shifted bisimilarity* – furnishes the basis for the representation of sets as types. In type-theoretic terms, a pointed graph may be defined as a triple (**A**, *R*, and *a*) with **A**, a type; *R*, a term of type $\mathbf{A} \to (\mathbf{A} \to \Omega)$; and *a*, a term of type **A**. The conditions for a bisimilarity between pointed graphs given previously – and so also the representation of set membership in terms of shifted bisimilarity – are then readily translated into the language of type theory. This yields a faithful interpretation of set theory within type theory under which sets correspond to pointed graphs and the membership relation corresponds to shifted bisimilarity.

2.4 Criticism of Ramified Types

To return to the historical record: after the publication of *Principia,* a number of mathematicians and logicians, notably Weyl, Chwistek, and Ramsey, identified technical deficiencies in it and attempted to remedy them. In *Das Kontinuum,*[35] Weyl presents a predicative formulation of mathematical analysis – not, as Russell and Whitehead had attempted, by introducing a hierarchy of logically ramified types, which Weyl seems to have regarded as too complicated and also as requiring the dubious Axiom of Reducibility[36] – but rather by confining the comprehension principle to formulas whose bound variables range over just the initial given entities (numbers). Accordingly, Weyl restricts analysis to what can be done in terms of natural numbers with the aid of three basic logical operations, together with the operation of substitution and the process of 'iteration', that is, primitive recursion. Weyl recognized that the effect of this restriction would be to render unprovable many of the central results of classical analysis[37] – for example, Dirichlet's principle that any bounded set of real numbers has a least upper bound – but he was prepared to accept this as part of the price that must be paid for the security of mathematics.

In 1925, Chwistek formulated what he called the theory of *constructive types.*[38] This is essentially the system of *Principia* purged of all existential propositions, including the Axiom of Reducibility. It has the property that each of its symbols can be obtained by the application of a finite number of

---

[35] Weyl (1918).

[36] In Weyl (1946), he remarks:

> *[The Axiom of Reducibility] is a bold, an almost fantastic axiom; there is little justification for it in the real world in which we live, and none at all in the evidence on which our mind bases its constructions.*

[37] This would also have been the case for a ramified type theory lacking the Axiom of Reducibility.

[38] Chwistek (1925).

operations applied to a set of initial symbols. Chwistek's system is, in fact, no stronger than that of Weyl.

The year 1926 saw the publication of Ramsey's important paper 'The Foundations of Mathematics'.[39] The core of Ramsey's paper is a critique of the logical system of *Principia Mathematica*, together with a proposal for setting it right. Ramsey identifies a number of defects in *Principia.* The first of these is that it admits only definable classes, in violation of 'the extensional attitude of modern mathematics', an essential part of which is 'the possibility of indefinable classes and relations in extension'. He continues:

> *The mistake is made not by having a primitive proposition asserting that all classes are definable, but by giving a definition of class which applies only to definable classes, so that all mathematical propositions about some or all classes are misinterpreted. This misinterpretation is not merely objectionable on its own account in a general way, but is especially pernicious in connection with the Multiplicative Axiom, which is a tautology when properly interpreted, but when misinterpreted after the fashion of* Principia Mathematica *becomes a significant empirical proposition, which there is no reason to suppose true.*

By the Multiplicative Axiom, Ramsey means the version of the Axiom of Choice asserting that for any non-empty family K of disjoint non-empty sets, there is a set having exactly one member in common with each set in K. Ramsey says that according to the extensional view, he takes of classes, 'the Multiplicative Axiom seems … the most evident tautology'. It only becomes really doubtful when 'the class whose existence it asserts must be one definable by a propositional function of the sort which occurs in *Principia*'. Ramsey shows that the Multiplicative Axiom (more precisely, its logical equivalent that the cardinalities of any pair of sets are comparable) can, in fact, be falsified in a *Principia*-like system in which there are very few atomic propositional functions.

Ramsey's chief objection against the theory of types presented in *Principia* is the fact that in order to become an adequate foundation for mathematics, it requires the introduction of the 'illegitimate' Axiom of Reducibility. Ramsey attributes this to the fact that the authors of *Principia* have failed to observe that the contradictions whose avoidance is one of the work's chief purposes actually fall into two 'fundamentally distinct' groups. The first of these, of which Russell's paradox is representative, 'consists of contradictions which, were no provision made against them, would occur in a logical or mathematical system itself'. They 'involve only logical or mathematical terms such as class and

[39] Ramsey (1926).

number, and show that there must be something wrong with our logic or mathematics'. On the other hand, the contradictions in the second group, of which the Liar Paradox and the Heterological Paradox are representative, 'are not purely logical, and cannot be stated in logical terms alone; for they all contain some reference to thought, language, or symbolism, which are not formal but empirical terms'. So 'they may be due not to faulty logic or mathematics, but to faulty ideas concerning thought and language'.

Ramsey points out that the theory of types actually consists of two distinct parts 'directed respectively against the two groups of contradictions', unified only by 'being both deduced in a somewhat sloppy way from the 'vicious circle principle'. But it is essential, he insists, to consider them separately. The contradictions in the first group can be eliminated by noting that a propositional function cannot meaningfully take itself as an argument, which leads to a division of 'functions and classes into a hierarchy of types according to their possible arguments'. As a result, there are functions of individuals, functions of functions of individuals, and so on. And then 'the assertion that a class is a member of itself is neither true nor false, but meaningless'. Ramsey regards this part of the theory of types – the part which would later evolve into the simple theory of types – as 'unquestionably correct'.

As for the second part of the theory, which is designed to contend with the second group of contradictions, it 'requires further distinctions between the different functions which take the same arguments'. These distinctions are reflected in the orders of *Principia*, the classification of functions according to the level of their bound variables. Ramsey agrees that the contradictions in the second group are circumvented by the introduction of orders, but this resolution 'lands us in an almost equally serious difficulty, for it invalidates many important mathematical arguments which appear to contain exactly the same fallacy as the contradictions'. To overcome this deficiency, the authors of *Principia* had introduced the Axiom of Reducibility, a postulate that in Ramsey's view 'there is no reason to suppose true', whose truth, indeed, would be merely 'a happy accident and not a logical necessity'. 'Such an axiom', Ramsey asserts, 'has no place in mathematics, and anything which cannot be proved without using it cannot be regarded as proved at all'.

Ramsey then considers the question of why the Axiom of Reducibility fails to reproduce the contradictions (those in the second group) the ramified theory of types was explicitly designed to avoid. In asserting that any function is coextensive with a predicative function, the Axiom of Reducibility 'may appear to lose again whatever was gained by making the distinction'. Ramsey says that the reason why these contradictions fail to reappear is their 'peculiar nature'. They 'are not purely mathematical, but all involve the ideas of thought or meaning'; in a word, they are *intensional.* If any purely mathematical contradictions were to arise from the conflating of arbitrary with predicative functions or from the identification of intensionally different but extensionally equivalent functions, then these contradictions would, says Ramsey, be 'reinstated by the Axiom of Reducibility, owing to the extensional nature of mathematics, in which [extensionally] equivalent functions are interchangeable'. The fact that no such contradictions have been shown to arise underscores the intensional nature of the contradictions in the second group, making it 'even more probable that they have a psychological or epistemological, and not a purely logical or mathematical solution'. Ramsey's conclusion is that 'there is something wrong with the account of the matter given in *Principia*'.

Ramsey's attitude towards the foundations of mathematics and logic was robustly extensional and accordingly realist. This realist attitude insulated him from the worries about impredicative definition that had exercised Russell (and Weyl). In Ramsey's view, the distinction of orders of functions is just a complication imposed by the structure of our language and not, unlike the hierarchy of types, something inherent in the way things truly are. Ramsey's suggestion in *The Foundations of Mathematics* for repairing the defects in *Principia* reflects his realist orientation. In essence, his proposal is to render the whole apparatus of orders superfluous through the simple expedient of eliminating quantifiers in definitions. Thus, a universal quantifier is regarded as indicating a conjunction, and an existential quantifier a disjunction, of the collection of propositions obtained from a given propositional function by the substitution of a name of any one of the members of the collection of objects – itself conceived as existing independently of any definition we might propose – which constitutes the propositional function's range of significance.[40] It does not matter whether it may be impossible in practice to write out the resulting expressions in full (indeed, these expressions may be of infinite length). Once the apparatus of orders is abandoned, a *simple* theory of types remains, similar to that which Russell had originally proposed for classes-as-many. Ramsey was convinced that the simple theory of types would provide an adequate foundation for mathematics.

Neither Chwistek nor Ramsey produced a detailed formulation of the simple theory of types, although it seems clear that either could have done this had he so wished. In fact, the first fully worked out formulation is that of Carnap (1929); later formulations include Tarski (1931) and Gödel (1931).

[40] On this reckoning, then, the statement ***Citizen Kane*** *has all the qualities that make a great film* would be taken as an abbreviation for something like ***Citizen Kane*** *is a film, brilliantly directed, superbly photographed, outstandingly performed, excellently scripted, etc.*

2.5 Church's Version of the Simple Theory of Types

The form of the simple theory of types that has proved definitive was put forward by Church (1940). Church's system is based on functions instead of relations or classes and incorporates certain features of the λ-*calculus* that had been previously developed by him. Church's system has had a profound influence on computer science, particularly in the areas of automated theorem proving, computational logic, and formal methods. Among logicians and computer scientists, Church-style systems based on the λ-calculus have become the most popular way of presenting type theories.[41]

A straightforward version of Church's simple type theory is the following system *T*. *T* is equipped with the *types* and *terms,* specified as follows:

Types: **I**, the type of individuals
$\mathbf{\Omega}$, the type of propositions or truth values
A collection of base types
Function types $(\mathbf{A} \to \mathbf{B})$, for any types **A, B** (we omit the parentheses whenever possible)

Terms: Terms are introduced according to the following rules so that each term t is assigned a type **A,** written t: **A.**

Variables $x_{\mathbf{A}}, y_{\mathbf{A}}, z_{\mathbf{A}}, \ldots$ of each type **A** (we omit the subscript whenever possible)
Individuals a, b, c, ... of type **I**
Function application. If t: **A** and $f : \mathbf{A} \to \mathbf{B}$, then $f(t)$: **B**
Function abstraction. If t: **B**, then $(\lambda x_{\mathrm{A}} \cdot t) : \mathbf{A} \to \mathbf{B}$
Equality. If t: **A**, u: **A**, then $t = u : \Omega$

Terms of type Ω are called *propositions* or *formulas.*

Notice that *T* lacks logical operators. It was observed by Henkin (1963) that they can in fact be defined in a system like *T*. Let ω and ω′ be variables of type $\mathbf{\Omega}$, and α and β be propositions. Then we can write

$\top$	for	$(\lambda\omega.\omega) = (\lambda\omega.\omega)$
$\bot$	for	$(\lambda\omega.\mathrm{T}) = (\lambda\omega.\omega)$
$\neg\alpha$	for	$\alpha = \bot$
$\alpha \Leftrightarrow \beta$	for	$\alpha = \beta$
$\alpha \wedge \beta$	for	$\lambda f \cdot f(\mathrm{T})(\mathrm{T}) = \lambda f \cdot f(\alpha)(\beta)$, with $f : \Omega \to (\Omega \to \Omega)$

41 It should be mentioned, however, that there is an alternative way of formulating type theories based on the *combinatory calculus* introduced by Curry in the 1930s. See Barendregt (1984, 1992) and Curry and Feys (1958).

(cont.)

$\alpha \Rightarrow \beta$	for	$\alpha \wedge \beta \Leftrightarrow \alpha$
$\forall x.\ \alpha$	for	$\lambda x.\ \alpha = \lambda x.\ \top$
$\alpha \vee \beta$	for	$\forall \omega[(\alpha \Rightarrow \omega) \wedge (\beta \Rightarrow \omega)] \Rightarrow \omega]$
$\exists x.\ \alpha$	for	$\forall \omega[\forall x(\alpha \Rightarrow \omega) \Rightarrow \omega]$

T can be furnished with both a semantics and a deductive apparatus similar to those for higher-order logic, and analogous theorems proved.[42]

A simple type theory like *T*, employing just function application, function abstraction, and equality, can serve as a foundation for mathematics in the sense that the usual mathematical structures, for example, the natural numbers and the reals, admit straightforward formulations within it. And with appropriate axioms (including an axiom of infinity to the effect that the type of individuals is infinite), it can be shown that simple type theory has the same proof-theoretic strength as bounded Zermelo set theory.

Church's formulation of the simple theory of types is evidently far from being a faute de mieux; it is, rather, the theory that naturally ensues from an analysis of the function concept. This is well summed up by Robin Gandy:

> *The simple theory of types provides a straightforward, reasonably secure foundation for the greater part of classical mathematics. This is why a number of authors (Carnap, Godel, Tarski, Church, Turing) gave a precise formulation of it, and used it as a basis for metamathematical investigations. The theory is straightforward because it embodies two principles which (at least before the advent of modern abstract concepts) were part of the mathematicians' normal code of practice. Namely that a variable always has a precisely delimited range, and that a distinction must always be made between a function and its arguments.*[43]

3 Local Set Theory

Another formulation of the simple theory of types emerged in the early 1970s from the work of Lawvere and Tierney[44] in the mathematical discipline known as *category theory*.[45] They introduced a certain kind of category they termed an *elementary topos*. It soon became clear that such categories can be associated with a natural version of simple type theory, but, unlike Church's version, based

[42] Benzmüller and Andrews (2019) and Farmer (2006). [43] Gandy (1977), p. 173.
[44] See Lawvere (1971, 1972).
[45] See Section **A.1** for a brief account of the basic ideas of category theory.

on *intuitionistic*, rather than classical logic. The system we shall describe here, *local set theory,* or *intuitionistic higher-order logic,*[46] is a modification, due to Zangwill (1977), of the system of Joyal and Boileau, later published as their (1981). It combines the most convenient features of simple type theory and set theory. Here, we give an abbreviated account of local set theory: a full account is given in Bell (1988).

3.1 Local Set Theory and Its Logic

A local set theory is a type-theoretic system built on the same primitive symbols =, $\in$, and {:} as classical set theory, in which the set-theoretic operations of forming products and powers of types can be performed and which in addition contains a 'truth value' type acting as the range of values of 'propositional functions' on types. A local set theory is determined by specifying a collection of *axioms* formulated within a *local language* defined as follows.

A *local language* $\mathscr{L}$ has the following *basic symbols:*

- **1** (*unit type*)
- **Ω** (*truth value type*)
- **S, T, U, ...** (*ground types*: possibly none of these)
- **f, g, h, ...** (*function symbols*: possibly none of these)
- $x_A, y_A, z_A, \ldots$ (*variables of each type* **A**, where a *type* is as defined later)
- ★ (*unique entity of type* **1**)

The *types* of $\mathscr{L}$ are defined recursively as follows:

- **1** and **Ω** are types.
- Any ground type is a type.
- $\mathbf{A}_1 \times \ldots \times \mathbf{A}_n$ is a type whenever $\mathbf{A}_1, \ldots, \mathbf{A}_n$ are types, where, if $n = 1$,
- $\mathbf{A}_1 \times \ldots \times \mathbf{A}_n$ is $\mathbf{A}_1$, while if $n = 0$, $\mathbf{A}_1 \times \ldots \times \mathbf{A}_n$ is **1** *(product types)*.
- **PA** is a type whenever **A** is (*power types*).

Each function symbol **f** is assigned a *signature* of the form $\mathbf{A} \rightarrow \mathbf{B}$, where **A** and **B** are types; this is indicated by writing $\mathbf{f}:\mathbf{A} \rightarrow \mathbf{B}$.

Terms of $\mathscr{L}$ and their associated *types* are defined recursively as follows. We write: **A** to indicate that the term τ has type **A.**

[46] Because of its category-theoretic origins, local set theory is also known as *higher-order categorical logic,* as in Lambek and Scott (1986).

Term: type	**Proviso**
$\bigstar: \mathbf{1}$	
$x_{\mathbf{A}}: \mathbf{A}$	
$\mathrm{f}(\tau): \mathbf{B}$	$\mathbf{f}: \mathbf{A} \to \mathbf{B}; \boldsymbol{\tau}: \mathbf{A}$
$<\tau_1, \ldots, \tau_n>: \mathbf{A_1} \times \ldots \times \mathbf{A}_n$, where $<\tau_1, \ldots, \tau_n>$ is τ_1 if $n = 1$ and $\bigstar$ if $n = 0$	$\tau_1 : \mathbf{A}_1, \ldots, \tau_n : \mathbf{A}_n$
$(\tau)i : \mathbf{A}_i$ where $(\tau)_i$ is τ if $n = 1$	$\tau : \mathbf{A_1} \times \ldots \times \mathbf{A}_n,\ 1 \leq i \leq n$
$\{x_{\mathbf{A}}: \alpha\}: \mathbf{PA}$	$\alpha: \mathbf{\Omega}$
$\sigma = \tau : \Omega$	σ and τ are of same type
$\sigma \in \tau$	σ: **A,** τ: **PA** for some type **A**

Terms of type $\mathbf{\Omega}$ are called *formulas, propositions,* or *truth values.* Notational conventions we shall adopt include:

ω, ω', and ω''	Variables of type Ω
α, β, and γ	Formulas
$x, y, z \ldots$	$x_{\mathbf{A}}, y_{\mathbf{A}}, z_{\mathbf{A}} \ldots$
$\tau(x/\sigma)$ or $\tau(\sigma)$	Result of substituting σ at each free occurrence of x in τ: an occurrence of x is *free* if it does not appear within $\{x\text{: } \alpha\}$
$\alpha \leftrightarrow \beta$	$\alpha = \beta$
Γ: α	*Sequent notation*: Γ a finite set of formulas, which could be the empty set $\varnothing$
$: \alpha$	$\varnothing : \alpha$

A term is *closed* if it contains no free variables; a closed term of type $\mathbf{\Omega}$ is called a *sentence.* Any local language is equipped with a *deductive apparatus* consisting of axioms and rules of inference formulated in terms of sequents.

The *basic axioms* for a local language $\mathscr{L}$ are as follows:

Unity	$:x_1 = \bigstar$
Equality	$:x = y, \alpha(z/x) : \alpha(z/y)$ (x, y free for z in α)
Products	$:(< x_1, \ldots, x_n >)_i = x_i$
	$: x = < (x)_1, \ldots, (x)_n >$
Comprehension	$:x \in \{x : \alpha\} \leftrightarrow \alpha$

The *rules of inference* for $\mathscr{L}$ are as follows:

Thinning $\quad \dfrac{\Gamma\text{: }\alpha}{\beta, \Gamma\text{: }\alpha}$

Restricted cut $\quad \dfrac{\Gamma\text{: }\alpha \quad \alpha, \Gamma\text{: }\beta}{\Gamma\text{: }\beta}$ (any free variable of a free in Γ or β)

Substitution $\dfrac{\Gamma: \alpha}{\Gamma(x/\tau) : \alpha(x/\tau)}$ (τ free for x in Γ and a)

Extensionality $\dfrac{\Gamma: x \in \sigma \leftrightarrow x \in \tau}{\Gamma: \sigma = \tau}$ (x not free in Γ, σ, and τ)

Equivalence $\dfrac{\alpha, \Gamma: \beta \quad \beta, \Gamma: \alpha}{\Gamma: \alpha \leftrightarrow \beta}$

These axioms and rules of inference yield a system of *natural deduction* in $\mathscr{L}$, generating *derivations* of sequents from collections of sequents. If *S* is any collection of sequents in $\mathscr{L}$, we say that the sequent $\Gamma : \alpha$ is *derivable from S* and write $\Gamma \vdash_S \alpha$, provided there is a derivation of $\Gamma : \alpha$ using just the basic axioms, the sequents in *S*, and the rules of inference. We shall also write $\Gamma \vdash \alpha$ for $\Gamma \vdash_{\emptyset} \alpha$ and $\vdash_S \alpha$ for $\emptyset \vdash_S \alpha$. If $\vdash_S \alpha$, we shall say that α is *provable* from *S*.

A formula α is called *refutable* in *S* if $\vdash_S \neg\alpha$. *S* is *consistent* if it is not the case that $\vdash_S \bot$. *S* is *complete* if each sentence is either provable or refutable from *s*.

A *local set theory,* or simply a *theory* in $\mathscr{L}$, is a collection *S* of sequents closed under derivability from *S*. Any collection of sequents *S generates* the local set theory *S** comprising all the sequents derivable from *S*. The local set theory in $\mathscr{L}$ generated by $\emptyset$ is called *pure* local set theory in $\mathscr{L}$.

Notice that no *logical operators* were included in the basic vocabulary of a local language. These are introduced by definition[47] as follows:

Logical Operator	**Definition**
T (true)	$\star = \star$
$\alpha \wedge \beta$	$< \alpha, \beta > = < \mathrm{T}, \mathrm{T} >$
$\alpha \rightarrow \beta$	$(\alpha \wedge \beta) \leftrightarrow \alpha$
$\forall x\ \alpha$	$\{x : \alpha\} = \{x : \mathrm{T}\}$
$\bot$ (false)	$\forall \omega.\ \omega$
$\neg\alpha$	$\alpha \rightarrow \bot$
$\alpha \vee \beta$	$\forall \omega[(\alpha \rightarrow \omega \wedge \beta \rightarrow \omega) \rightarrow \omega]$
$\exists x\ \alpha$	$\forall \omega[\forall x(\alpha \rightarrow \omega) \rightarrow \omega]$

We also write $x \neq y$ for $\neg(x = y)$, $x \notin y$ for $\neg\ (x \in y)$, and $\exists! x\ \alpha$ for $\exists x[\alpha \wedge \forall y\ \alpha(x/y) \rightarrow x = y]$.

What system of logical laws do these operators satisfy? That is, what logical system is generated by the deductive apparatus of local set theory?

[47] The definition of logical operators given here is similar to that presented in Section **2.5.**

It turns out that the system in question is the so-called *free first-order intuitionistic logic*. This is obtained from the system of first-order classical logic laid out in Section 1.3 by suppressing axiom (x)[48] and restricting applications of the rule of inference *modus ponens* $\alpha, \alpha \to \beta/\beta$ to cases in which *all free variables of a are also free in β*.[49] By constructing the appropriate derivations, it can be shown that the axioms of free first-order intuitionistic logic are provable and its rules of inference derivable within local set theory. (These derivations in local set theory are omitted here but are presented in detail in Bell (1998).)

This fact that is often expressed by saying that the 'internal logic' of local set theory is intuitionistic.

3.2 Set Theory in a Local Language

We next introduce the concept of *set* in a local language. A *set-like* term is a term of power type; a *closed* set-like term is called an ($\mathscr{L}$ -) *set.* We shall use upper case italic letters $X, Y, Z, \ldots$ for sets, as well as standard abbreviations such as $\forall x \in X.\alpha$ for $\forall x(x \in X \to \alpha)$. The set-theoretic *operations* and *relations* are defined as follows. Note that in the definitions of $\subseteq$, $\cap$, and $\cup$, *X* and *Y must be of the same type:*

Operation	Definition
$\{x \in X: \alpha\}$	$\{x: x \in X \wedge \alpha\}$
$X \subseteq Y$	$\forall x \in X.\, x \in Y$
$X \cap Y$	$\{x: x \in X \wedge x \in Y\}$
$X \cup Y$	$\{x: x \in X \vee x \in Y\}$
$x \notin X$	$\neg(x \in X)$
$U_{\mathbf{A}}$ or A	$\{x_{\mathbf{A}} : \top\}$
$\emptyset_{\mathbf{A}}$ or $\emptyset$	$\{x_{\mathbf{A}} : \bot\}$
$E - X$	$\{x: x \in E \wedge x \notin X\}$
PX	$\{u: u \subseteq X\}$
$\cap U$ (U: **PPA**)	$\{x: \forall u \in U.\, x \in u\}$
$\cup U$ (U: **PPA**)	$\{x: \exists u \in U.\, x \in u\}$
$\bigcap_{i \in I} X_i$	$\{x : \forall i \in I.\, x \in X_i\}$
$\bigcup_{i \in I} X_i$	$\{x : \exists i \in I.\, x \in X_i\}$

[48] Axiom (x) is the *law of double negation.*

[49] The restriction on modus ponens is imposed to allow for the possibility that type **A** may be empty in the sense that no closed term of type A may exist. In this case, the sentence $\exists x_{\mathrm{A}}(x_{\mathrm{A}} = x_{\mathrm{A}})$ will not be provable. This is the source of the use of the term 'free' – it is an abbreviation for the phrase 'free of existential assumptions'.

(cont.)

Operation	Definition
$\{\tau_1, \ldots, \tau_n\}$	$\{x : x = \tau_1 \vee \ldots \vee x = \tau_n\}$
$\{\tau : \alpha\}$	$\{z : \exists x_1 \ldots \exists x_n(z = \tau \wedge \alpha)\}$
$X \times Y$	$\{<x,y>: x \in X \wedge y \in Y\}$
$X + Y$	$\{<\{x\},\varnothing>: x \in X\} \cup \{<\varnothing,\{y\}.: y \in Y\}$
$Fun(X,Y)$	$\{u: u \subseteq X \times Y \wedge \forall x \in X\, \exists! \in Y <x,y> \in u\}$

The following facts concerning the set-theoretic operations and relations may now be established as straightforward consequences of their definitions:

(i) $\vdash X = Y \leftrightarrow \forall x(x \in X \leftrightarrow x \in Y)$

(ii) $\vdash X \subseteq X, \vdash (X \subseteq Y \wedge Y \subseteq X) \rightarrow X = Y,$

$\vdash (X \subseteq Y \wedge Y \subseteq Z) \rightarrow X \subseteq Z$

(iii) $\vdash Z \subseteq X \cap Y \leftrightarrow Z \subseteq X \wedge Z \subseteq Y$

(iv) $\vdash X \cup Y \subseteq Z \leftrightarrow X \subseteq Z \wedge Y \subseteq Z$

(v) $\vdash x_A \in U_A$

(vi) $\vdash \neg(x \in \varnothing_{\mathbf{A}})$

(vii) $\vdash X \in PY \leftrightarrow X \subseteq Y$

(viii) $\vdash X \subseteq \cap U \leftrightarrow \forall u \in U \cdot X \subseteq u$

(ix) $\vdash \cup U \subseteq X \leftrightarrow \forall u \in U.u \subseteq X$

(x) $\vdash x \in \{y\} \leftrightarrow x = y$

(xi) $\vdash \alpha \rightarrow \tau \in \{\tau : \alpha\}$

Here, (i) is the *axiom of extensionality*, (iv) the *axiom of binary union,* (vi) the *axiom of the empty set*, (vii) the *power set axiom*, (ix) the *axiom of unions*, and (x) the *axiom of singletons.* These, together with the comprehension axiom, form the core axioms for set theory in L. The set theory is *local* because some of the set-theoretic operations, for example, intersection and union, may be performed only on sets of the same type, that is, 'locally'. Moreover, variables and quantifiers are constrained to range only over given types – 'locally' – in contrast with the situation in classical set theory where they are permitted to range globally over an all-embracing universe of discourse. And, as we have already pointed out, the logic governing these 'local' quantifiers is intuitionistic.

Given a term τ such that

$<x_1, \ldots, x_n> \in X \vdash_S \tau \in Y.$

we write$(<x_1, \ldots, x_n> \mapsto \tau)$ or simply $\boldsymbol{x} \mapsto \tau$ for

$\{<<x_1, \ldots, x_n>, \tau : <x_1, \ldots, x_n> \in X\}.$

Clearly, we have

$$\vdash_S (<x_1, \ldots, x_n> \mapsto \tau)) \in Fun(X, Y),$$

and so we may think of $(<x_1, \ldots, x_n> \mapsto \tau)$ as the function from X to Y determined by τ.

Let S be a local set theory in a local language $\mathscr{L}$. Define the relation $\approx_S$ on the collection of all $\mathscr{L}$-sets by

$$X \approx_S Y \text{ iff } \vdash_S X = Y.$$

This is an equivalence relation. An *S-set* is an equivalence class $[X]_S$ – which we normally identify with X – of $\mathscr{L}$-sets under the relation $\approx S$. An *S-map* $f : X \to Y$ is a triple *(f, X, Y)* – normally identified with f – of *S*-sets such that $\vdash_S f \in Y^X$. X and Y are, respectively, the *domain* dom(*f*) and the *codomain* cod (*f*). Any pair of maps $f : X \to Y$ and $g : Y \to Z$ can be *composed* to yield a map $g \circ f : X \to Z$ given by

$$g \circ f = \{<x, z>: \exists y(<x, y> \in f \wedge <y, z> \in g)\}.$$

S-sets and *S*-maps constitute a *category,* the *category of S*-sets, denoted by **C**(*S*). This category can be shown to be an elementary topos. For further details, see Section A.3.

3.3 Classicality and the Choice Principle

We have observed that the internal logic of a local set theory is intuitionistic. It is a remarkable fact that postulating the Axiom of Choice (mentioned in Section **2.3**) forces the logic to become classical, that is, to satisfy the Law of Excluded Middle: for any proposition *p, p,* or $\neg p$, or, equivalently, the Law of Double Negation $\neg\neg p \to p$[50].

Let S be a local set theory in a language $\mathscr{L}$. We make the following.

Definitions

- S is *classical* if $\vdash_S \forall\omega(\omega \vee \neg\omega)$. This is the full Law of Excluded Middle for S.
- S is *sententially classical* if $\vdash_S \alpha \vee \neg\alpha$ for any sentence α. This is a weakened form of the Law of Excluded Middle.
- S is *choice* if for any *S*-sets *X, Y* and any formula a with at most the variables *x, y* free the following rule (the *choice rule*[51]) is valid:

[50] This is axiom (x) of the system of classical first-order logic laid out in Section **1.3**.

[51] The choice rule is a formal version of the 'functional' version of the Axiom of Choice mentioned in footnote 29.

$$\frac{\vdash_S \forall x \in X \exists y \in Y\ \alpha(x,y)}{\vdash_S \forall x \in X\ \alpha(x, fx) \text{ for some } f: X \to Y}.$$

- An S-set X is *discrete* if

$$\vdash_S \forall x \in X\ \forall y \in X. x = y \vee x \neq y.$$

- A *complement* for an S-set X **: PA** is an S-set Y**: PA** such that

$$\vdash_S X \cup Y = A \wedge X \cap Y = \varnothing.$$

An S-set that has a complement is said to be *complemented.*

Here are some facts concerning these notions.

1. *Any of the following conditions is equivalent to the classicality of S:*

(i) $\vdash_S \Omega = \{\top, \bot\}$.
(ii) *S satisfies the Law of Double Negation,* that is, $\vdash_S \neg\neg\omega \to \omega$.
(iii) *any S-set is complemented.*
(iv) *any S-set is discrete.*
(v) *Ω is discrete.*

Proof. (iii) If S is classical, clearly, $\{x: x \notin X\}$ is a complement for X. Conversely, if $\{\top\}$ has a complement U, then

$$\vdash_S \omega \in U \to \neg(\omega = \top) \to \neg\omega \to \omega = \bot.$$

Hence, $\vdash_S U = \{\bot\}$, from which $\vdash_S \Omega = \{\top\} \cup U = \{\top, \bot\}$.

(v) If Ω is discrete, then $\vdash_S \omega = \top \vee \neg(\omega = \top)$, so $\vdash_S \omega \vee \neg\omega$.

Diaconescu's Theorem.[52] *Any choice local set theory is classical.*

Proof. Step 1. *S choice $\Rightarrow$ S_I choice for any S-set I.*

Proof of step 1. Suppose that S is choice, and

$$\vdash_{S(I)} \forall x \in X(c)\ \exists y \in Y(c) \alpha(x, y, c).$$

Then

$$\vdash_S \forall x \in X(i)\ \exists y \in Y(i) \alpha(x, y, i).$$

[52] This is the version, for local set theories, of Diaconescu's (1975) theorem that any topos in which the Axiom of Choice holds is Boolean. Step 2 of the proof employs the argument used by Goodman and Myhill (1978) to prove the set-theoretic version of the theorem.

Define

$$X^* = \{<x, i>: x \in X(i) \wedge i \in I\},\ Y^* = \bigcup_{i \in I} Y(i)$$

$$\beta(u, i) \equiv \exists x \in X(i) \exists i \in I[u = <x, i> \wedge \alpha(x, y, i) \wedge y \in Y(i)].$$

Then

$$\vdash ts\ \forall u \in X^* \exists y \in Y^* \beta(u, y).$$

So choice yields $f^*: X^* \to Y^*$ such that

$$\vdash_S \forall u \in X^* \beta(u, f^* u).$$

That is,

$$\vdash s \forall i \in I \forall x \in X(i)\, \alpha(x, f^*(<x, i>, i) \wedge f^*(<x, i>) \in Y(i)],$$

from which

$$\vdash ts\ \forall x \in X(c) \alpha(x, f^*(<xc>, c) \wedge f^*(<x, c>\ ) \in Y(c)].$$

Now define $f = (x \mapsto f * (<x, c>))$. Then $f: X(c) \to Y(c)$ in S_I and

$$\vdash s(I)\ \forall x \in X(c) \alpha(x, fx, c).$$

This completes the proof of step 1.

Step 2. *S choice* $\Rightarrow$ *S sententially classical.*

Proof of step 2. Define $2 = \{0, 1\}$ and let $X = \{u \subseteq 2 : \exists y \cdot y \in u\}$. Then

$$\vdash s \forall u \in X \exists y \in 2 \cdot y \in u.$$

So, by choice, there is $f: X \to 2$ such that

$$\vdash s \forall u \in X \cdot fu \in u.$$

Now let α be any sentence; define

$$U = \{x \in 2 : x = 0 \vee \alpha\}, V = \{x \in 2 : x = 1 \vee \alpha\}.$$

Then $\vdash_S U \in X \wedge V \in X$, so, writing $a = fU, b = fV$, we have

$$\vdash s[a = 0 \vee \alpha] \wedge [b = 1 \vee \alpha].$$

from which

$$\vdash_S [a = 0 \wedge b = 1] \vee \alpha,$$

so that

$$(*) \quad \vdash_s a \neq b \vee \alpha.$$

But $\alpha \vdash_S U = V \vdash_S a = b$ so that $a \neq b \vdash_S \rightarrow \alpha$. It follows from this and (*) that

$$\vdash_s \alpha \vee \neg\alpha,$$

as claimed. This establishes step 2.

Step 2 establishes that ***if pair sets have choice functions, then logic is classical.***

Step 3 (obvious). *S classical* $\Leftrightarrow$ *S*Ω *sententially classical.*

Finally, to prove Diaconescu's theorem, we observe that

$$S \text{ choice} \Rightarrow S_\Omega \text{ choice} \Rightarrow S_\Omega \text{ sententially classical} \Rightarrow S \text{ classical}.$$

The proof is complete.

3.4 The Natural Numbers in Local Set Theory

Let S be a theory in a local language $\mathscr{L}$. A *natural number system in S* is a triple (**N**, ***s***. $\underline{0}$), consisting of a type symbol **N**, a function symbol $s : \mathbf{N} \rightarrow \mathbf{N}$ and a closed term $\underline{0}\,|\mathbf{N}$, satisfying the following *Peano axioms*.

(P1) $\vdash_S sn \neq \underline{0}$

(P2) $sm = sn \vdash_s m = n$

(P3) $\underline{0} \in u, \forall n(n \in u \rightarrow sn \in u) \vdash_S \forall n\,.\, n \in u$

Here, m and n are variables of type **N**; u is a variable of type **PN**; and we have written ***sn*** for ***s***(n). (P3) is the *axiom of induction.*

In a local set theory S with a natural number system, $\underline{0}$ is called the *zeroth numeral.* For each natural number $n \geq 1$, the *n-th numeral* $\underline{n}$ in S is defined recursively by putting $\underline{n} = \mathbf{s}(\underline{n-1})$. Numerals are closed terms of type **N** that may be regarded as *formal representatives* in S of the natural numbers.

It is readily shown that (P3) is equivalent to the following *induction scheme:*

For any formula, α *with exactly one free variable of type* **N**, *if* $\vdash_S \alpha(\underline{0})$ *and* $\alpha(n)$ $\vdash_S \alpha(sn)$, then $\vdash_S \forall\, n\, \alpha(n)$.

Peano arithmetic may be formulated as a local set theory in the following way.

Let $\mathscr{L}_{\mathbf{N}}$ be the local language with just one ground type symbol **N**, one function symbol $s : \mathbf{N} \to \mathbf{N}$, and one function symbol $\boldsymbol{0} : \mathbf{1} \to \mathbf{N}$. Write $\underline{0}$ for $\boldsymbol{0}$ (★). Let P be the theory in $\mathscr{L}_{\mathbf{N}}$ generated by the sequents

$$: sn \neq \underline{0}$$

$$sm = sn : m = n$$

$$\underline{0} \in u, \forall n(n \in u \to sn \in u) : \forall n.n \in u$$

where m and n are variables of type **N** and u is a variable of type **PN**. The triple (**N**, s, and $\underline{0}$) is then a natural number system in P. The theory P is called *Peano arithmetic.*

P has certain features that make it attractive from a constructive standpoint: for instance, it has both the *disjunction property,* namely, for sentences β and γ

$$\vdash_P \beta \vee \gamma \Leftrightarrow \vdash_p \beta \text{ or } \vdash_P \gamma,$$

and is *witnessed,* that is,

if $\vdash_P \exists m\ \alpha\ (m)$, then, for some numeral $\underline{n}$, $\vdash_P \alpha(m/\underline{n})$.

3.5 Tarski and Godel's Theorems in Local Set Theory

The famous theorems of Tarski and Gödel on the undefinability of truth and incompleteness in formal theories have elegant general formulations within local set theory. Here, we give a brief outline.

Let $\mathscr{L}$ be a local language containing a type symbol **C**, which we shall call the *type of codes of formulas:* letters u and v will be used as variables of type **C** and the letter **u** will denote a closed term of type **C**. We shall also suppose that $\mathscr{L}$ contains formulas $\tau(u)$ and $\delta(u.v)$, and for each formula $\alpha(u)$, containing at most the free variable u, a closed term $\ulcorner\alpha\urcorner$ called the *code* of α. The assignment $\alpha \rightsquigarrow \ulcorner\alpha\urcorner$ is called the *coding map.* A local language satisfying these conditions will be called *codable.*

Let S be a theory in a codable language $\mathscr{L}$. We say that

- δ is a *diagonal relation* in S if

$$\vdash_S \forall v \delta(\ulcorner\alpha\urcorner, v) \leftrightarrow v = \ulcorner\alpha(\ulcorner\alpha\urcorner)\urcorner \text{ for any formula } \alpha(u)$$

- is a *truth definition* for S if

$$\vdash_S \tau(\ulcorner\alpha\urcorner) \leftrightarrow \alpha \text{ for any sentence } \alpha.$$

Since ↔ is the same as =, a truth definition thus amounts to a (sentence-by-sentence) *left inverse* to the coding map.

- τ is a *demonstration predicate* for *S* if
  $\vdash_S \alpha \Leftrightarrow \; \vdash_S \tau(\ulcorner\alpha\urcorner)$ for any sentence α.

We first prove the:

Fixed Point Lemma. Suppose that *S* is a theory in a codable language with a diagonal operator. Then any formula $\alpha(u)$ has a 'fixed point', that is, there is a sentence β such that

$$\vdash_S \beta \leftrightarrow \alpha(\ulcorner\beta\urcorner).$$

Proof. Let δ be a diagonal relation in *S;* given $\alpha(u)$, write $\gamma(u)$ for the formula $\exists v[\delta(u,v) \wedge \alpha(v)]$; let **u** be the term $\ulcorner\gamma\urcorner$; and define β to be the sentence $\gamma(\mathbf{u})$, that is, $\gamma(\ulcorner\gamma\urcorner)$. Because δ is a diagonal relation, we have

(1) $\forall v\delta(\ulcorner\gamma\urcorner, v) \leftrightarrow v = \ulcorner\gamma(\ulcorner\gamma\urcorner)\urcorner$.

Then, using (1), we have

$$\begin{aligned}\vdash_S \beta &\leftrightarrow \gamma(\ulcorner\gamma\urcorner)\\ &\leftrightarrow \exists v[\delta(\ulcorner\gamma\urcorner v) \wedge \alpha(v)]\\ &\leftrightarrow \exists v[v = \ulcorner\gamma(\ulcorner\gamma\urcorner)\urcorner \wedge \alpha(v)](\text{by } (1)\\ &\leftrightarrow \alpha(\ulcorner\gamma(\ulcorner\gamma\urcorner)\urcorner)\\ &\leftrightarrow \alpha(\ulcorner\beta\urcorner),\end{aligned}$$

as required.

We use this to prove:

Tarski's Theorem. Let *S* be a theory in a codable language with a diagonal relation. Then if *S* has a truth definition, it is inconsistent, that is, $\vdash_S \bot$.

Proof. Let δ be a diagonal relation in *S* and τ a truth definition for *S.* Let β be a fixed point for the formula $\neg\tau(\mathrm{u})$; thus,

(1) $\vdash_S \beta \leftrightarrow \neg\tau(\ulcorner\beta\urcorner)$.

Since τ is a truth definition for *S*, we have

(2) $\vdash_S \beta \leftrightarrow \tau(\ulcorner\beta\urcorner)$.

Now (1) and (2) give $\vdash_S \bot$, that is, *S* is inconsistent.

It follows that a consistent codable local set theory with a diagonal relation cannot have a truth definition.

Recall that a local set theory *S* is *complete* if each sentence is either provable or refutable from *S.*

We next prove:

Gödel's First Incompleteness Theorem. Let S be a theory in a codable language with a diagonal relation. Then if S is consistent and has a demonstration predicate, it is incomplete.

Proof. The proof is similar to that of Tarski's theorem. Let δ be a diagonal relation in S and τ a demonstration predicate for S. Let β be a fixed point for the formula $\neg\tau(u)$; thus,

$$(1)\quad \vdash_S \beta \leftrightarrow \neg\tau(\ulcorner\beta\urcorner).$$

Since τ is a demonstration predicate for S we have

$$(2)\quad \vdash_S \beta \Leftrightarrow \vdash_S \tau(\ulcorner\beta\urcorner).$$

From (1) and (2): it follows that

$$(2)\quad \vdash_S \tau(\ulcorner\beta\urcorner) \Leftrightarrow \vdash_S \beta \Leftrightarrow \vdash_S \neg\tau(\ulcorner\beta\urcorner).$$

So if S is consistent, the sentence $\tau(\ulcorner\beta\urcorner)$ is neither provable nor refutable in S, that is, S is incomplete.

In order to formulate Gödel's second incompleteness theorem in local set theory, we require the following definition:

- τ is a *proof predicate* for S if it satisfies, for any sentences α, β,

(a) $\vdash_S \alpha \Rightarrow \vdash_S \tau(\ulcorner\alpha\urcorner)$,
(b) $\tau(\ulcorner\alpha \rightarrow \beta\urcorner) \vdash_S \tau(\ulcorner\alpha\urcorner) \rightarrow \tau(\ulcorner\beta\urcorner)$,
(c) $\tau(\ulcorner \tau(\ulcorner\alpha\urcorner)\text{l}) \vdash_S \tau(\ulcorner\alpha\urcorner)$.

If τ is a proof predicate, we shall write $\Box\alpha$ for $\tau(\ulcorner\alpha\urcorner)$. Then $\Box$ is a *provability operator*, that is, satisfies

(a′) $\vdash_S \alpha \Rightarrow \vdash_S \Box\alpha$,

(b′) $\Box(\alpha \rightarrow \beta) \vdash_S \Box\alpha \rightarrow \Box\beta$, and

(c′) $\Box\alpha \vdash_S \Box\Box\alpha$.

It is readily shown that

(d′) $\alpha \vdash_S \beta \Rightarrow \Box\,\alpha \vdash_S \Box\,\beta$ and

(e′) $\vdash_S \alpha \leftrightarrow \beta \Rightarrow \vdash_S \Box\,\alpha \leftrightarrow \Box\beta$.

Let us call a theory in a codable language *adequate* if it has both a diagonal relation and a proof predicate.

We prove:

Lob's Theorem. Suppose that S is an adequate theory. Then for any sentence α,

(i) $\Box(\Box\alpha \rightarrow \alpha) \vdash s\ \Box\alpha$,
(ii) $\neg\Box\alpha \vdash s \neg\Box\neg\Box\alpha$, and
(iii) $\Box\alpha \vdash s\ \alpha \Rightarrow\ \vdash s\ \alpha$.

Proof. (i) Applying the fixed point lemma to the formula $\tau(u) \rightarrow \alpha$ yields a sentence β for which

$$\vdash s\ \beta \leftrightarrow (\tau(\ulcorner\beta\urcorner) \rightarrow \alpha),$$

that is,

$$(1)\quad \vdash s\ \beta \leftrightarrow (\Box\beta \rightarrow \alpha).$$

It follows that

$$\vdash s\ \beta \leftrightarrow (\Box\beta \rightarrow \alpha),$$

from which by (b′)

$$\vdash s\ \Box\beta \rightarrow \Box(\Box\beta \rightarrow \alpha).$$

Hence, again using (b′)

$$(2)\quad \Box\beta \vdash s \Box(\Box\beta \rightarrow \alpha) \vdash s\ \Box\Box\beta \rightarrow \Box\alpha.$$

Then, since by (c′) $\Box\beta \vdash s\ \Box\Box\beta$, it follows from (2) that

$$(3)\quad \Box\beta \vdash s \Box\alpha,$$

from which $\Box\alpha \rightarrow \alpha \vdash s\ \Box\beta \rightarrow \alpha$. Hence, by (d′)

$$(4)\quad \Box(\Box\alpha \rightarrow \alpha) \vdash s\ \Box(\Box\beta \rightarrow \alpha).$$

It now follows from (1) and (e′) that $\vdash s\ \Box\beta \leftrightarrow \Box\ (\Box\beta \rightarrow \alpha)$, and from this and (4), we obtain $\Box(\Box\alpha \rightarrow \alpha) \vdash s\ \Box\ \beta$. This, together with (3), gives $\Box(\Box\alpha \rightarrow \alpha) \vdash s$ $\Box\alpha$, that is, (i).

(ii) Using (i),

$$\Box\neg\Box\ \alpha_{\vdash s}\ \Box(\Box\alpha \rightarrow\ \bot) \vdash s\ \Box(\Box\ \alpha \rightarrow \alpha) \vdash s\ \Box\alpha.$$

Hence, $\neg\ \Box\alpha + s\neg\Box\neg\Box\alpha$.

(ii) Suppose $\Box\ \alpha \vdash s\ \alpha$. Then $\vdash s\ \Box\alpha \rightarrow \alpha$ and so, by (a′) $\vdash s\Box(\Box\alpha \rightarrow \alpha)$. From this and (i), it follows that $\vdash s\ \Box\alpha$.

From (i) of Löb's theorem, we see that $\Box$ provably satisfies the so-called *GL* (Gödel–Löb) *axiom* for a normal modal logic, that is, the scheme

$\Box(\Box A \to A) \to \Box A$.

Corollary. The following conditions are equivalent for an adequate theory *s:*

(i) For any sentence α, $\alpha \vdash_S \neg\neg\Box\ \alpha$.
(ii) For any sentence α, $\vdash_S \neg\neg\Box\ \alpha$.
(iii) $\vdash_S \neg\neg\Box\ \bot$.

A fortiori $\alpha \vdash_S \neg\neg\Box\ \alpha$ for all sentences α implies $\vdash_S \neg\neg\Box\ \bot$.

Proof. (i) $\Rightarrow$ (ii). Suppose $\alpha \vdash\ s \neg\neg\Box\ \alpha$ for any sentence α. Then in particular

(1) $\neg\ \Box\alpha \vdash\ s \neg\neg\Box\ \neg\Box\alpha$.

By (ii) of Löb's theorem,

(2) $\neg\ \Box\alpha \vdash_S \neg\Box\neg\Box\alpha$.

From (1) and (2), it follows that $\neg\ \Box\alpha \vdash_S \bot$, from which $\vdash_S \neg\neg\ \Box\alpha$.

(ii) $\Rightarrow$ (iii) is trivial.

(iii) $\Rightarrow$ (i). Suppose $\vdash_S \neg\neg\Box\bot$. Now for any sentence α, $\vdash_S \neg\neg\Box\bot \to \neg\neg\Box\alpha$. It follows that $\vdash_S \neg\neg\ \Box\alpha$ so that $\alpha \vdash\ s \neg\neg\Box\alpha$.

The sentence $\neg\Box\bot$, that is, $\neg\tau(\ulcorner\bot\urcorner)$, expresses, with respect to the proof predicate τ, the unprovability within *S* of $\bot$, that is, the *internal consistency* of *s*. From Löb's theorem, one derives:

Gödel's Second Incompleteness Theorem. Suppose that *S* is consistent and adequate. Then, for any sentence α, it is not the case that $\vdash_S \neg\Box\alpha$. In particular, the sentence expressing the internal consistency of *S* is not provable in *s*.

Proof. Suppose that $\vdash_S \neg\Box\alpha$, that is, $\vdash_S \Box\alpha \to \bot$. Since $\vdash_S \bot \to \alpha$, it follows that $\vdash_S \Box\bot \to \Box\alpha$, and hence, $\vdash_S \Box\bot \to \bot$. It follows from Löb's theorem that $\vdash_S \bot$, that is, *S* is inconsistent.

The second incompleteness theorem may be taken to assert that in an adequate consistent theory, *there is no proposition whose unprovability is provable.*

The idea of internal consistency can be extended to the following concordance:

Proposition	Meaning
$\Box\bot$	*S is internally inconsistent.*
$\neg\Box\bot$	*S is internally consistent.*
$\neg\neg\Box\bot$	*S is weakly internally inconsistent.*
$\Box\neg\Box\bot$	*S is provably internally consistent.*
$\neg\Box\neg\Box\bot$	*S is not provably internally consistent.*

In each case, the claim that the proposition is provable in S is correlated with an assertion about S: for example, $\neg\Box\bot$ with the assertion 'S is internally inconsistent' and similarly for the others.

In this spirit, consider a special case of (ii) of Löb's theorem, namely, the inequality $\neg\Box\bot \vdash_S \neg\Box\neg\Box\bot$. This may be paraphrased: in S, *internal consistency implies the unprovability of internal consistency.* This is an *internal version* of Gödel's second incompleteness theorem.

In this same spirit, the previously provided Corollary translates as: if, in S, every proposition implies its own provability, then S is weakly internally inconsistent.

Notice that *consistency and internal inconsistency are compatible.* This follows from the fact that the provability predicate $\tau(u)$ can be taken to be the formula $u = u$ so that every proposition can be taken to satisfy the internal condition '*__ is provable*'. All this shows is that internal consistency need have little to do with consistency or, more generally, that provability maps need have little to do with provability.

Finally, consider Peano arithmetic as formulated as the theory P in the language $\mathscr{L}_{\mathbf{N}}$ above. This language can be rendered codable as follows: take $\mathbf{N}$ to be the type of codes, and for each formula α, take $\ulcorner\alpha\urcorner$ to be the numeral $\underline{n}$, where n is the Gödel number of α under some standard Gödel numbering of the expressions of $\mathscr{L}_{\mathbf{N}}$. It is known[53] that all primitive recursive functions and relations are representable in P so that, in particular, the diagonal map $\alpha(u)\mapsto\ulcorner\alpha(\ulcorner\alpha\urcorner)\urcorner$ and the proof relation of formulas in P are both representable therein. Take $\delta(m,n)$ to be the formula of $\mathscr{L}_{\mathbf{N}}$ representing in P the diagonal map and let $Prf(m, n)$ be a formula in $\mathscr{L}_{\mathbf{N}}$ representing in P the provability relation, namely, '*m is the Godel number of a proof in P of the formula with Godel number n*'. Finally, take $\tau(n)$ to be the formula $\exists m Prf(m, n)$.

This prescription ensures that δ is a diagonal relation in P. Also, $\tau(n)$ is a demonstration predicate. To see this, suppose that α is a sentence with Gödel

[53] This is proved in Lambek and Scott (1986).

number n and $\vdash_{FITT} \alpha$. Then there is a proof of a in *P*. Let m be the Gödel number of such a proof. Then since *Prf* represents the provability relation in *P*, it follows that $\vdash_P Prf(\underline{m}, \underline{n})$, i.e., $\vdash_P Prf(\underline{m}, \ulcorner\alpha\urcorner)$. It follows that $\vdash_p \exists m Prf(m, \ulcorner\alpha\urcorner)$, i.e. $\vdash_P \tau(\ulcorner\alpha\urcorner))$. Conversely, suppose that $\vdash_P \tau(\ulcorner\alpha\urcorner)$, i.e $\vdash_P \exists m Prf(m, \ulcorner\alpha\urcorner)$. Then for some numeral $\underline{m}$, $\vdash_P Prf\left(\underline{m_2}, \ulcorner\alpha\urcorner\right)$. Since *Prf* represents the provability relation in *P*, it follows that m is the Gödel number of a proof in P of α, from which $\vdash_P \alpha$.

From all this, we deduce that P is subject to Gödel's first incompleteness theorem, namely, that if P is consistent, it is incomplete.

It can also be shown that the formula $\tau(n)$ as just defined is a proof predicate in P so that P is adequate. Accordingly, P satisfies Gödel's second incompleteness theorem, that is, if P is consistent, the sentence expressing its internal consistency is unprovable therein.

4 Newer Forms of Type Theory Based on the Doctrine of 'Propositions as Types'

4.1 The Doctrine of Propositions as Types and Constructive Dependent Type Theory

Type theory took a remarkable turn in the 1980s with the emergence of the *propositions as types* doctrine. Underlying this doctrine is the idealist notion, traceable to Kant and central to Brouwerian intuitionism, that the meaning of a proposition does not derive from an absolute standard of truth external to the mind but resides rather in the evidence for its assertability in the form of a mental construction or proof. The central thesis of the 'propositions-as-types' doctrine (*PATD* for short) is that each proposition is to be *identified* with the type, set, or assemblage of its proofs.[54] As a result, such proof types, or sets of proofs, have to be accounted the *only* types, or sets, that are present. *PATD* thus embodies the idea that a type, or set, simply *is* the type, or set, of proofs of a proposition, and reciprocally, a proposition *is* just the type, or set, of its proofs.

In a simple type theory or a local set theory, each type is independent of other types and is thus, so to speak, absolute or static; this holds in particular of the type of propositions or truth values. Now, formulas or propositional functions in general manifest variation, since their values vary over, or depend on, the domain(s) of their free variables. Because of this, they cannot be accurately represented as static types. This limitation makes it impossible for a simple type theory to realize faithfully the doctrine of propositions as types. For this to

[54] This idea was advanced by Curry and Feys (1958) and later by Howard (1980). As the *Curry-Howard correspondence*, it has come to play an important role in theoretical computer science.

become possible, it is necessary to develop a theory of 'variable' or *dependent* types, wherein types can depend on, or 'vary over', other types. In a dependent type theory, type symbols may take the form **B**(x), with x a variable of a given type **A**. **B**(x) is then a type dependent on or varying over the type **A.**

Such a theory – *constructive dependent type theory* (CDTT)[55] – was formulated[56] by Per Martin-Löf (1975, 1982, 1984). Since its introduction, CDTT has come to play a significant role both in the foundations of mathematics and in theoretical computer science.

CDTT is the first truly constructive theory of types, in the sense of being both predicative (so in particular lacking a type of propositions[57]) and based on intuitionistic logic. In formulating it, Martin-Löf's purpose was to provide, as he put it in Martin-Löf (1975) 'a full-scale system for formalizing intuitionistic mathematics as developed, for example, in the book by Bishop'.[58] Martin-Löf's system provides a complete embodiment of *PATD*.[59] Here is Martin-Löf himself on the latter in Martin-Löf (1975):

> *Every mathematical object is of a certain kind or type. Better, a mathematical object is always given together with its type, that is it is not just an object: it is an object of a certain type. ... A type is defined by prescribing what we have to do in order to construct an object of that type ... Put differently, a type is well-defined if we understand.what it means to be an object of that type. Note that it is required, neither that we should be able to generate somehow all the objects of a given type, nor that we should so to say know all of them individually. it is only a question of understanding what it means to be an arbitrary object of the type in question. A proposition is defined by prescribing how we are allowed to prove it, and a proposition holds or is true intuitionistically if there is a proof of it. ... Conversely, each type determines a proposition, namely, the proposition that the type in question is non-empty. This is the proposition which we prove by exhibiting an object of the type in question. On this analysis, there appears to be no fundamental difference between propositions and types. Rather, the difference is one of point of view: in the case of a proposition, we are not so much interested in what its proofs are as in whether it has a proof, that is, whether it is true or false, whereas, in*

55 CDTT is also known as *Martin-Löf type theory.*

56 Dependent types were actually first studied in the late 1960s by de Bruijn and his colleagues at the University of Eindhoven in connection with the AUTOMATH project.

57 The presence of a type of propositions would automatically justify the formulation of impredicatively defined propositions such as 'all propositions are assertable'.

58 That is, Bishop (1967). In his book, Bishop formulates a radically constructive approach to mathematical analysis, eschewing all parts of the discipline that cannot be ascribed concrete 'numerical meaning'.

59 Martin-Löf's original calculus contained a type of all types. This assumption was shown to be inconsistent by Girard (1972). Martin-Löf accordingly dropped this assumption in later versions of his theory.

the case of a type, we are of course interested in what its objects are and not only in whether it is empty or non-empty.

A key element in Martin-Löf's formulation of type theory is the distinction, which goes back to Frege, between *propositions* and *judgements*. Propositions (which in Martin-Löf's systems are identified with types) are syntactical objects on which mathematical operations can be performed and which bear certain formal relationships to other syntactical objects called *proofs*. Propositions and proofs are, so to speak, *objective* constituents of the system. Judgements, on the other hand, typically involve the *idealist* notion of 'understanding' or 'grasping the meaning of'. Thus, for example, while $2+2=4$ is a proposition, '$2+2=4$ is a proposition' and '$2+2=4$ is a true proposition' are judgements.

Martin-Löf also follows Frege in taking the rules of inference of logic to concern judgements rather than propositions. Thus, for example, the correct form of the rule of $\rightarrow$ -elimination is not

$$\frac{A \quad A \rightarrow B}{B}$$

but

$$\frac{A \text{ true} \quad A \rightarrow B \text{ true}}{B \text{ true}}.$$

That is, the rule does not say that proposition B follows from propositions A and $A \rightarrow B$, but that the *truth* of proposition B follows from the *truth* of proposition A conjoined with that of $A \rightarrow B$. In general, judgements may be characterized as expressions that appear at the conclusions of rules of inference.

Another important respect in which Martin-Löf follows Frege is in his insistence that judgements and formal rules be accompanied by full explanations of their *meaning*. (This is to be contrasted with the usual model-theoretic semantics that is really nothing more than a translation of one object language into another.) In particular, the judgement *A is a proposition* may be made only when one knows what a (canonical) proof of A is, and the judgement *A is a true proposition* only when one knows how to find such a proof. Judgements, and the notion of truth, are thus seen to be mind-dependent.

Martin-Löf's various systems abound in subtle distinctions. For example, in addition to the distinction between proposition and judgement, there is a parallel distinction between *type* (or set) and *category*[60] (or species).

[60] In this usage, of course, to be distinguished from the term as employed in its mathematical sense in Section 3 and the Appendix.

In order to be able to judge that A is a category, one must be able to tell what kind of objects fall under it and to judge when they are equal. To be in a position to make the further judgement that a category is a type, or set, one must be able to specify what its 'canonical' or typical elements are. In judging something to be a set, one must possess sufficient information concerning its elements to enable quantification over it to make sense. Thus, for example, the natural numbers form a type, with canonical elements given by: 0 is a canonical element of $\mathbb{N}$, and if n is a canonical element of $\mathbb{N}$, then $n+1$ is a canonical element of $\mathbb{N}$. On the other hand, the collection of subsets of $\mathbb{N}$ forms a category but not a set.

In CDTT, logical rules are introduced as procedures for producing correct judgements from earlier judgements.

First-order reasoning is presented using a single kind of judgement:

proposition B is true under the hypothesis that propositions $A_1, \ldots, A_n$ are all true.

This *hypothetical judgement* is written as a *sequent*

$$\mathbf{A}_1, \ldots, \mathbf{A}n \vdash \mathbf{B}.$$

When $n = 0$, then the *categorical judgement* $\vdash \mathbf{B}$ states that $\mathbf{B}$ is true without any assumptions.

CDTT has four basic forms of judgement.

The four forms of *categorical* judgement are:

- $\vdash \mathbf{A}$ type. meaning that $\mathbf{A}$ is a well-formed type;
- $\vdash a : \mathbf{A}$, meaning that the term a has type $\mathbf{A}$;
- $\vdash \mathbf{A} = \mathbf{A}'$, meaning that $\mathbf{A}$ and $\mathbf{A}'$ are equal types; and
- $\vdash a = a' : \mathbf{A}$, meaning that a and a' are (judgementally) equal elements of type $\mathbf{A}$.

In general, a judgement is *hypothetical*, that is, it is made in a context Γ, that is, a list $x_1 : \mathbf{A}_1, \ldots, x_n : \mathbf{A}_n$ of variables that may occur free in the judgement together with their respective types. The four basic forms of hypothetical judgements are then $\Gamma \vdash \mathbf{A}$ type, $\Gamma \vdash a : \mathbf{A}$, and $\Gamma \vdash a = a' : \mathbf{A}$. Under the proposition as types interpretation $\vdash a : \mathbf{A}$ can be understood as the judgement that a is a proof of proposition $\mathbf{A}$.

CDTT contains the important *rule of type equality*:

$$\frac{\Gamma \vdash a : \mathbf{A} \ \Gamma \vdash \mathbf{A} = \mathbf{B}}{\Gamma \vdash a : \mathbf{B}}.$$

Rules for the logical operators will be discussed in the following section.

4.2 Logical Operators and Type Operations in Constructive Dependent Type Theory

PATD gives rise to a correspondence between logical operators and operations on (dependent) types. We shall present the idea in set-theoretic terms.[61] As above, we write a: **A** to indicate that the object a is of type **A.** Objects of type **A** will also be called *elements* of **A.** A type is *inhabited* if it has an element. Thus, if the type is construed as a proposition, it is inhabited precisely when the associated proposition has a proof, and if it is construed as a set, then it is inhabited precisely when the associated set is non-empty.

Now consider two propositions/types/sets **A** and **B**. What should be required of a proof f of the implication $\mathbf{A} \to \mathbf{B}$? Just that, given any proof x of **A**, f should yield a proof of **B**, that is, f should be a function from **A** to **B**. In other words, proposition $A \to B$ is just the type of functions from **A** to **B**:

$$\mathbf{A} \to \mathbf{B} = \mathbf{B}^{\mathbf{A}}.$$

Similarly, all that should be required of a proof c of the conjunction $\mathbf{A} \wedge \mathbf{B}$ is that it should yield proofs x and y of **A** and **B**, respectively. From this point of view, $\mathbf{A} \wedge \mathbf{B}$ is just the type $\mathbf{A} \times \mathbf{B}$ of all pairs (x, y), with x: **A** and y: **B**.

A proof of the disjunction $\mathbf{A} \vee \mathbf{B}$ is either a proof of **A** or a proof of **B** together with the information as to which of **A** or **B**, it is a proof. That is, if we introduce the type **2** with the two distinct elements 0 and 1, a proof of $\mathbf{A} \vee \mathbf{B}$ may be identified as a pair (c, n) in which either c is a proof of **A** and n is 0, or c is a proof of **B** and
n is 1. This means that $\mathbf{A} \vee \mathbf{B}$ should be construed as the disjoint union $\mathbf{A} + \mathbf{B}$ of **A** and **B**.

The true proposition T may be identified with the one element type $\mathbf{1} = \{0\}$: 0 thus counts as the unique proof of T. The false proposition $\perp$ is taken to be a proposition that lacks a proof altogether: accordingly, $\perp$ is identified with the empty set $\emptyset$. The negation $\neg\mathbf{A}$ of a proposition **A** is defined as $\mathbf{A} \to \perp$, which therefore becomes identified with the set $\emptyset^{A}$.

As we have already said, a proposition A is deemed to be true if it (i.e., the associated type **A**) has an element, that is, if there is a function $\mathbf{1} \to \mathbf{A}$. Accordingly, the *Law of Excluded Middle* for a proposition A becomes the assertion that there is a function $\mathbf{1} \to \mathrm{A} + \emptyset^{\mathbf{A}}$.

[61] Following Tait (1994).

If a and b are objects of type **A**, we introduce the *identity* (or *equality*) *type* $a =_{\mathbf{A}} b$, also written as $\mathbf{Id}_{\mathbf{A}}(a, b)$, expressing that a and b are identical, or equal, objects of type **A.** To assert that the proposition associated with $\mathbf{Id}_{\mathrm{A}}(a, b)$ is true is to assert that the $\mathbf{IdA}(a, b)$ is inhabited, which informally means that a and b are identical. $\mathbf{Id}_{\mathbf{A}}$ is a dependent type, varying over the type $\mathbf{A} \times \mathbf{A}$. Objects $p\colon a =_{\mathbf{A}} b$ or $p\colon \mathbf{Id}_{\mathrm{A}}(a, b)$ represent the various ways in which a and b can be identified, and so $a =_{\mathbf{A}} b$ or $\mathbf{Id}_{\mathrm{A}}(a, b)$ is also known as the *type of identifications* of a and b.[62]

In order to deal with the quantifiers, we require operations defined on families of types, that is, types $\mathbf{\Phi}(x)$ depending on objects x of some type **A**. By analogy with the case $\mathbf{A} \to \mathbf{B}$, a proof f of the proposition $\forall x{:}\mathbf{A}\ \mathbf{\Phi}(x)$, that is, an object of type $\forall x{:}\mathbf{A}\ \mathbf{\Phi}(x)$, should associate with each $x\colon \mathbf{A}$ a proof of $\mathbf{\Phi}(x)$. So f is just a function with domain A such that for each $x\colon \mathbf{A}$, fx is of type $\mathbf{\Phi}(x)$. That is, $\forall x\colon \mathbf{A}\ \mathbf{\Phi}(x)$ is the *product* $\prod x\colon \mathbf{A}\ \mathbf{\Phi}(x)$ of the $\mathbf{\Phi}(x)$'s. We use the λ-notation in writing f as $\lambda x f x$.

A proof of the proposition $\exists x{:}\mathbf{A}\ \mathbf{\Phi}(x)$, that is, an object of type $\exists x{:}\mathbf{A}\ \mathbf{\Phi}(x)$, should determine an object $x\colon \mathbf{A}$ and a proof y of $\mathbf{\Phi}(x)$, and vice versa. So a proof of this proposition is just a pair (x, y) with $x\colon \mathbf{A}$ and $y\colon \mathbf{\Phi}(x)$. Therefore, $\exists x{:}\mathbf{A}\ \mathbf{\Phi}(x)$ is the *disjoint union,* or *coproduct* $\coprod x{:}\mathbf{A}\ \mathbf{\Phi}(x)$ of that of the $\mathbf{\Phi}(x)$.

To translate all this into the language of CDTT, one uses the following concordance:

Logical Operation	**Set-Theoretic Operation**	**Type-Theoretic Operation**
$\wedge$	$\times$	$\times$
$\vee$	$+$	Two-term dependent sum
$\to$	Set exponentiation	Type exponentiation
$\forall x$	Cartesian product $\prod_{i \in I}$	Dependent product $\prod x{:}\mathbf{A}$
$\exists x$	Disjoint union $\coprod_{i \in I}$	Dependent sum $\coprod x\colon \mathbf{A}$

In CDTT, each of these type-theoretic operations is supplied with a list of rules for its use.[63] To illustrate, here are the formation and elimination rules for $\prod$ (which corresponds to the universal quantifier $\forall$). We write

[62] The possibility that an identity type may have more than one element, that is, objects may be identified in more than one way, makes identity in CDTT *intensional* in the sense of footnote 16. An *extensional* version of CDTT can be obtained by introducing a rule ensuring that the elements of identity types are judgementally equal.

[63] For a complete specification of the operations and rules of CDTT, see chapter 10 of Jacobs (1999) or Gambino and Aczel (2005).

$\mathbf{B}[x/a]$ for the result of substituting the term a for each free occurrence of the variable x in $\mathbf{B}$.

$\prod$ – formation:

$$\frac{\Gamma \vdash \mathbf{A} \quad \Gamma, x: \mathbf{A} \vdash \mathbf{B}}{\Gamma \vdash \Pi x: \mathbf{A}.\mathbf{B}}.$$

$\prod$ – elimination:

$$\frac{\Gamma \vdash f: \Pi x: \mathbf{A}.\mathbf{B} \quad \Gamma \vdash a: \mathbf{A}}{\Gamma \vdash fa: \mathbf{B}[x/a]}.$$

In addition to admitting type operations corresponding to logical operations, CDTT also allows the construction of *inductive types*.[64] These are types $\mathbf{A}$ whose elements are 'freely generated' by the application of specified functions f: $\mathrm{A}^{\mathbf{A}}$. The natural number type $\mathbf{N}$ is an example: here, one is given the data 0: $\mathbf{N}$, s: $\mathbf{N}^{\mathrm{N}}$, with s the successor function. The elements of $\mathbf{N}$ are then 0, $s0$, $ss0$, ….

4.3 The Axiom of Choice in Constructive Dependent Type Theory

Of especial interest is the status of the *Axiom of Choice* in CDTT. We introduce the functions σ, π, and π' of types $\forall x$: $\mathbf{A}(\mathbf{\Phi}(x) \rightarrow \exists x$: $\mathbf{A}\mathbf{\Phi}(x))$, $\exists x$: $\mathbf{A}\varphi(x) \rightarrow \mathbf{A}$, and $\forall y$: $(\exists x\, \mathbf{\Phi}(x))$. $\mathbf{\Phi}(\pi(y))$ as follows. If b: $\mathbf{A}$ and c: $\mathbf{\Phi}(b)$, then σbc is (b, c). If d: $\exists x$:$\mathbf{A}$ $\mathbf{\Phi}(x)$, then d is of the form (b, c) and in that case $\pi(d) = b$ and $\pi'(d) = c$. These yield the equations

$$\pi(\sigma bc) = b \quad \pi'(\sigma bc) = c \quad \sigma(\pi d)(\pi' d) = d.$$

We may take the Axiom of Choice as proposition

(AC) $\forall x$: $\mathbf{A}\exists y$: $\mathbf{B}\mathbf{\Phi}(x,y)) \rightarrow \exists f$: $\mathbf{B}^{\mathbf{A}}\forall x$: $\mathbf{A}\mathbf{\Phi}(x,fx))$.

Remarkably, **AC** is correct under *PATD*, that is, *provable* in CDTT, as the following argument shows. Let u be a proof of the antecedent $\forall x$:$\mathbf{A}\exists y$:$\mathbf{B}$ $\mathbf{\Phi}(x, y))$. Then, for any x: $\mathbf{A}$, $\pi'(ux)$ is of type $\mathbf{B}$ and $\pi'(ux)$ is a proof of $\mathbf{\Phi}(x, \pi ux)$. So $s(u) = \lambda x.\pi(ux)$ is of type $\mathbf{B}^{\mathbf{A}}$ and $t(u) = \lambda x.\, \pi'(ux)$ is a proof of $\forall x$:$\mathbf{A}$ $\mathbf{\Phi}(x, s(u)x)$. Accordingly, $\lambda u.\, \sigma s(u)t(u)$ is a proof of $\forall x$:$\mathbf{A}\exists y$:$\mathbf{B}$ $\mathbf{\Phi}(x,y)) \rightarrow \exists x$:$\mathbf{B}^{\mathbf{A}}\forall x$:$\mathbf{A}\mathbf{\Phi}(x,fx))$.

Put informally, what this shows is that in CDTT, the consequent of **AC** means *nothing more than its antecedent.* Indeed, in many versions of constructive mathematics, the assertability of an alternation of quantifiers $\forall x \exists y R(x,y)$ means *precisely* that one is given a function f for which $R(x,fx)$ holds for all x.[65]

64 See chapter 5 of Homotopy (2013).

65 It is for this reason that in fully constructive mathematics, the Axiom of Choice does not imply the Law of Excluded Middle.

We note that in ordinary set theory, the above argument establishes the *isomorphism* of the sets $\prod x$: $\mathbf{A}\coprod y$:$\mathbf{B}$ $\mathbf{\Phi}(x, y)$) and $\coprod f$:$\mathbf{B^A}$ Πx:$\mathbf{A}$ $\mathbf{\Phi}(x, fx)$) but not the validity of the usual Axiom of Choice. In set theory, **AC** is not represented by this isomorphism but is rather (equivalent to) the equality in which Π is replaced by $\bigcap$ and $\amalg$ by $\bigcup$, namely,

$$\bigcap_{x\in A}\bigcup_{y\in B}\Phi(x,y) = \bigcup_{f\in B^\wedge}\bigcap_{x\in A}\Phi(x,fx).$$

While in CDTT, **AC** is provable, and so a fortiori has no 'untoward' logical consequences, in intuitionistic set theory, this is far from being the case, as Diaconescu's theorem shows, in the latter, **AC** implies the law of excluded middle. In other words, **AC** interpreted as in *PATD* is tautologous,[66] but when construed in intuitionistic type theory, it is far from being tautologous, since its affirmation there yields classical logic. This prompts the question: what modification needs to be made to the *PATD* paradigm so as to yield the intuitionistic type-theoretic interpretation of **AC**? An illuminating answer to this question has been given by Maietti (2005) through the use of so-called *monotypes*, that is, (dependent) types containing at most one entity or having at most one proof. Thus, in a type theory, type **A** is a monotype if given a: **A** and b: **A,** the type $\mathbf{Id_A}$ (a, b) is inhabited. (In set theory, monotypes are *singletons*, that is, sets containing at most one element.) Maietti has shown that if one takes propositions to correspond to monotypes, rather than to arbitrary types, then **AC** reverts to its usual interpretation in intuitionistic type theory and so is no longer provable. Call this new interpretation the 'propositions-as-monotypes' interpretation.

Now let us reconsider **AC** under the 'propositions-as-monotypes' interpretation within set theory itself. It will be convenient to rephrase **AC** as the assertion

$$(*)\quad \forall i\in I\exists j\in JM_{ij} \leftrightarrow \exists f\in J^I\forall i\in IM_{iff(i)},$$

where $<M_{ij}: i \in I, j\in J>$ is any doubly indexed family of propositions. In the 'propositions as types' interpretation, (*) corresponds to the existence of an isomorphism between $\prod_{i\in I}\coprod_{j\in J} M_{ij}$ and $\coprod_{f\in J^I}\prod_{i\in I} M_{if(i)}$

[66] Precisely as Ramsey (*v* . *supra*) asserted but in this case for quite different reasons. Ramsey construed, and accepted the truth of, the Axiom of Choice as asserting the objective existence of choice functions, given extensionally and so independently of the manner in which they might be described. But the intensional nature of constructive mathematics and, in particular, of CDTT decrees that nothing is given completely independently of its description. This leads to a strong construal of the quantifiers which, as we have observed, trivializes the Axiom of Choice by rendering the antecedent of the implication constituting it essentially equivalent to the consequent. It is remarkable that the Axiom of Choice can be considered tautological both from an extensional and from an intensional point of view.

$$(**)\quad \bigcap_{i\in I}\bigcup_{j\in J} M_{ij} = \bigcup_{f\in J^I}\bigcap_{i\in I} M_{if(i)}.$$

On the other hand, if we think of each *Mij* as a set, then AC interpreted in the usual way can be presented in the form of the distributive law.

In the 'propositions-as-types' interpretation, the universal quantifier $\forall i\in I$ corresponds to the product $\prod_{i\in I}$ and the existential quantifier $\exists i\in I$ to the coproduct, or disjoint sum, $\prod_{i\in I}$ Now in the 'propositions-as-monotypes' interpretation, wherein propositions correspond to singletons, $\forall i\in I$ continues to correspond to $\prod_{i\in I}$, since the product of singletons is still a singleton. But the interpretation of $\exists i\in I$ is changed. In fact, the interpretation of $\exists i\in I\ M_i$ (with each M_i a singleton) now becomes $[\prod_{i\in I} M_i]$, where for each set X, $[X] = \{u : u = 0 \wedge \exists x.x \in X\}$ is the *canonical singleton* associated with X.

It follows that under the 'propositions-as-monotypes' interpretation, proposition $\forall i \in I \exists j \in J M_{ij}$ is interpreted as the singleton

$$(1)\quad \prod_{i\in I}\left[\coprod_{j\in J} M_{ij}\right],$$

and proposition $\exists f \in J^I \forall i \in I M_{if(i)}$ as the singleton

$$(2)\quad \left[\coprod_{f\in J^I}\prod_{i\in I} M_{if(i)}\right].$$

Under the 'propositions-as-monotypes' interpretation, **AC** would be construed as asserting the existence of an isomorphism between (1) and (2).

Now it is readily seen that to give an element of (1) amounts to no more than affirming that for every $i \in I$, $\bigcup_{j\in J} M_{ij}$ is non-empty. But to give an element of (2) amounts to specifying maps $f \in J^I$ and g with domain I such that $\forall i \in I g(i) \in M_{if(i)}$. It follows that to assert the existence of an isomorphism between (1) and (2), that is, to assert **AC** under the 'propositions-as-monotypes' interpretation, is tantamount to asserting **AC** in the form (**), so leading, via Diaconescu's theorem, to classical logic. This is in sharp contrast with **AC** under *PAT*, where, as we have seen, its assertion is automatically correct and so has no non-constructive consequences.

4.4 Sets in Constructive Dependent Type Theory

There is a purely *internal* way of defining the *set concept* in CDTT. To do this, it will be convenient to adopt the 'propositions-as-monotypes' interpretation and simply *identify* propositions with monotypes, thus defining a proposition to be type **A** for which we have $\mathbf{Id}_{\mathbf{A}}(a,b)$ for any elements a and b of **A.** Accordingly, a proposition is a type that has at most one element, which amounts to restricting the term 'proposition' to 'proposition admitting at most one proof'. This suggests a natural way of defining the concept of set in CDTT. We shall call type **A** a *set* if the type $\mathbf{IdA}(a,b)$ is a proposition for any elements a and b of **A**. Thus, a set is a type in which, for any pair of elements, there is at most one proof of the identity of the two.[67]

The concept of set leads to the concept of groupoid in CDTT. type **A** is a *groupoid* if the type $\mathbf{IdA}(a,b)$ is a set for any elements a and b of **A**. Here, the term 'groupoid' is appropriate because it can be shown, using just the rules of CDTT, that any type **A** satisfying this condition can be regarded as a groupoid in the categorical sense (see **A.1**) in which the objects are the elements of **A**, and the arrows between a and b are the elements of the *set* $\mathbf{IdA}(a,b)$. The composition of arrows is the proof that equality is transitive, and the identity arrow is the proof of reflexivity of equality. The invertibility of each arrow follows that from the stipulation that equality is a symmetric relation. The uniformity of the steps in forming the pattern *proposition* → *set* → *groupoid* suggests that it can be iterated. Thus, we can define a 2-*groupoid* to be a type **A** such that $\mathbf{IdA}(a,b)$ is a groupoid for any elements a and b of **A** a 3-*groupoid* to be a type **A** such that $\mathbf{IdA}(a,b)$ is a 2-groupoid for any elements a and b of **A** and so on. This yields an infinite ladder of types: propositions, sets, 2-groupoids, … 3-groupoids. In this way, CDTT can be seen as an extension of the realm of propositions and sets to a vast hierarchy of higher-type entities.

It is natural to ask what form of *axiomatic set theory* is interpretable in CDTT. This has been worked out by Peter Aczel[68] and has become come known as *constructive set theory* (CST). This is a system of intuitionistic set theory in which the set-theoretic operations reflect those on types in CDTT. In particular, CST will admit products and exponentials of sets. But, given the predicative nature of CDTT, CST must also be predicative. This means, in particular, that in CST, there can be no set of propositions and no power sets.

A particularly illuminating form of CST[69] employs the distinction between sets and classes, as in Gödel–Bernays set theory. In this version of CST, any predicate determines a class, but only certain classes are sets. Here, a class may be thought of as something like a species or category in Martin-Löf's sense, that is, a range of objects all of which share a given property, and whose identity relations are fully determinate, but whose 'extent' is not sufficiently fixed to admit quantification over it. A set, on the other hand, is a class with a fully determinate extent, hence supporting quantification. In CST, the class P*A* of all

[67] It is consistent with CDTT that *every type is a set.* See Escardo (2018).
[68] See bibliographic entries under Aczel, Aczel and Gambino, and Aczel and Rathjen.
[69] See Aczel and Rathjen (2001).

subsets – the power class – of set A is almost never a set (the only exception being the power class of the empty set). On the other hand, the exponential A^B of two sets A and B – the class of maps from B to A – is always a set, so in particular 2^A is always a set. In classical set theory, 2^A is essentially the power set of A, which cannot be the case in CST. This means that in CST, 2 cannot represent, as it does in classical set theory, the set of propositions or truth values. In classical set theory, 2 is P1, the power set of a one-element set, but in CST, P1, while of course a class, is not a set. It can be shown that classical set theory is equivalent to CST augmented by the law of excluded middle and the assertion that P1 is a set.

4.5 Other Forms of Type Theory

Other forms of type theory that have emerged in recent decades include *polymorphic type theory* that admits the presence of *type variables* so that a type variable ***X*** may occur inside type **A(*X*).** The assignment of 'types' to *type* variables (or terms) is achieved by the introduction of a new order of entities called *kinds*. Just as each ordinary term is assigned a type, so each type term is assigned a kind. In particular, there is a kind called **Type** that represents the 'kind of all types'.[70] Any type **A** then satisfies the judgement **A: Type**, and **Type** itself satisfies the judgement **Type: Kind**. In addition to **Type**, the presence of arbitrarily arbitrary 'subkinds' of **Type** may be assumed. It is also assumed that **Kind** is closed under the operations corresponding to Cartesian product and exponentiation and that **Type** is closed under these latter and those corresponding to product and sum over type variables of an arbitrarily given kind.

Polymorphic and dependent type theories have been combined in various ways. One form is the *calculus of constructions* of Coquand and Huet (1988). This has been extended to what Jacobs (1999) calls *full higher-order dependent type theory*, or the *full theory* for short. In dependent type theory, types can 'depend on' types; in polymorphic type theory, types can 'depend on' kinds. In the full theory, the dependence is extended to the remaining possibilities: those of kinds on types and kinds on kinds. An account of this, and other amalgamations of polymorphic and dependent type theories, may be found in Jacobs (1999).

4.6 Homotopy Type Theory

We conclude our discussion of type theory with a brief account of important recent development, *Homotopy Type Theory*.[71] This is an

[70] This is, of course, not the same as asserting that there is a *type* of all types, for to do so would be to rekindle Girard's paradox (see footnote 59).

[71] See Homotopy (2013). Also see Awodey(2017) and Shulman (2017).

interpretation – the *homotopy interpretation* – of dependent type theory in which types are thought of as (topological) spaces and identity types correspond to path spaces in homotopy theory. This new interpretation of the type concept in Homotopy Type Theory has suggested an equally new approach to the foundations of mathematics called *Univalent Foundations.* A surprising feature of Homotopy Type Theory is that mathematical proofs formulated within it are easily translated into a computer programming language, opening the way for computers to check the correctness of difficult proofs.

Homotopy theory is a branch of topology; the mathematical discipline concerned with spaces and continuous mappings between them. The basic notions of homotopy theory are these. A *homotopy* between a pair of continuous maps $f{:}X \rightarrow Y$ and $gX \rightarrow Y$ is a continuous map $H{:}X \times [0,1] \rightarrow Y$[72] satisfying $H(x,0) = f(x)$ and $H(x,1) = g(x)$. The homotopy H may be thought of as 'continuous deformation' of f into g. Two maps are *homotopic* if there is a homotopy between them. The spaces X and Y are said to be *homotopy equivalent,* written $X \simeq Y$, if there are continuous maps $X \rightarrow Y$ and $Y \rightarrow X$ whose composites are homotopic to the respective identity maps, that is, if X and Y are isomorphic 'up to homotopy'. Homotopy equivalent spaces are said to have the same *homotopy type.*

Given two points a and b of a space X, a *path* from a to b is a continuous map $p{:}[0,1] \rightarrow X$ such that $p(a) = 0$ and $p(1) = b$. In this case, we write p: $a \rightsquigarrow b$. The *path space* of X is the space $X^{[0,1]}$ of all paths in X.

In Homotopy Type Theory,[73] types are interpreted as spaces (up to homotopy) and the assertion a: **A** – *a is of type* **A** – is thought of as meaning 'a is a point of space **A**'. A function f : $\mathbf{A} \rightarrow \mathbf{B}$ is regarded as a continuous map of space **A** to space **B.**

The central idea of Homotopy Type Theory is that the logical notion of identity $a{=}_{\mathbf{A}}b$ of two objects a, b: **A** of the same type **A** can be understood as the existence of a path p: $a \rightsquigarrow b$ from point a to point b in **A.** The identity type $\mathbf{Id}_{\mathbf{A}}$ is correlated with the path space of **A**, and an object p: $\mathbf{Id}_{\mathbf{A}}$ (a,b) with a path p: $a \rightsquigarrow b$ in **A.**

Here is a table[74] correlating the different interpretations of type-theoretic concepts:

[72] Here, [0, 1] is the unit interval on the real line.

[73] The idea of a homotopy interpretation of type theory occurred independently to Voevodsky, and Awodey and Warren (2009).

[74] Taken (with some modifications) from Homotopy (2013, introduction).

Types	Logic	Sets	Homotopy
A	Proposition	set	Space (up to homotopy)
a: **A**	Proof	element	point
B(x)	Predicate	family of sets	fibration
$b(x)$: **B**(x)	conditional proof	family of elements	section
0, 1	⊥ (false), T (true)	∅, {∅}	∅, ★ (one-point space)
A + **B**	**A** ∨ **B**	disjoint union	coproduct space
A × **B**	**A** ∧ **B**	set of pairs (product)	product space
A → **B**	**A** ⇒ **B**	set of functions	function space
∐x:**A** **B**(x)	∃x:**A** **B**(x)	disjoint union	total space
∏x:**A** **B**(x)	∀x:**A** **B**(x)	product	space of sections
$\mathbf{Id_A}$	equality =	{(x, x): x ∈ **A**}	path space $\mathbf{A}^{[0,1]}$

In Homotopy Type Theory, propositions[75] correspond to contractible spaces, that is, spaces homotopically equivalent to a one-point space, while sets correspond to spaces that are homotopically equivalent to a discrete space.[76]

In Homotopy Type Theory, the introduction of inductive types is extended to the formation of *higher inductive types*[77] in which not only are new type elements generated, but also new instances of the corresponding identity types.

The most important new formal principle arising from the homotopy interpretation of type theory is Voevodsky's[78] far-reaching *Univalence Principle,* which asserts, in a certain sense, that isomorphic structures can actually be *identified.* In a nutshell, the idea underlying the Univalence Principle is this. Set theory is often formulated in terms of the notion of *class,* and sets themselves are identified as 'small' classes – classes that can themselves be members of classes. In such formulations of set theory, there is a class V called the *universal class* whose members are all sets. (V itself cannot be a set on pain of contradiction.) Similarly, type theory allows the introduction of the idea of a 'small' type and the presence of a *universal type* **U** whose objects are all small types. As with any type, **U** has an identity type $\mathbf{Id_U}$, which represents the identity relation **A** = **B** between small types: $\mathbf{Id_U}(\mathbf{A}, \mathbf{B})$ is the type of identifications of **A** and **B.**

---

[75] Recall that a proposition is now taken to be a monotype: a type **A** for which we have $\mathbf{Id_A}(a,b)$ for any elements a, b of **A**.

[76] A space satisfying this condition may be pictured as a bunch of separate 'blobs', each of which can be shrunk to a distinct point, resulting in a discrete space.

[77] See chapter 6 of Homotopy (2013). [78] Voevodsky (2015).

Now, the notion of *equivalence* between types can be formulated within type theory, giving rise to a new defined type **Equiv(A, B)** of *equivalences* between **A** and **B.** The Univalence Principle then asserts that *there is an equivalence between the types* $\mathbf{Id}_{\mathrm{U}}(\mathbf{A}, \mathbf{B})$ *and* **Equiv(A, B)**.

Now we can define a map $f: \mathbf{A} \to \mathbf{B}$ to be an *equivalence*,[79] if, for every element b of **B**, the type of pairs (a,p), where p is of type $\mathbf{Id}_{\mathrm{B}}(fa, b)$, is a proposition and is inhabited. This explicitly asserts that any element of **B** is the image of a unique element of **A** so that, in particular, we recover the usual notion of a bijection between sets. For any equivalence $f: \mathbf{A} \to \mathbf{B}$, there is a function f^* $\mathbf{B} \to \mathbf{A}$ that can be thought of as the inverse of f. It can then be shown that the identity map on **A** is an equivalence. Let **Equiv(A,B)** be the type of pairs $(f p)$ where $f: \mathbf{A} \to \mathbf{B}$ and p is a proof that f is an equivalence. The fact that the identity map is an equivalence yields an element of **Equiv(A,A)** for any type **A.** Using this, a specific function i: $\mathbf{Id}_{\mathrm{U}}(\mathbf{A}, \mathbf{B}) \to$ **Equiv(A,B)** may be constructed[80] within type theory. This is a formal expression of the assertion that *identical types are equivalent.* Now the *Univalence Principle* asserts that *i is an equivalence.* Assuming the Univalence Principle, we have the function $i^*: \mathbf{Equiv}(\mathbf{A}, \mathbf{B}) \to \mathbf{Id}_{\mathrm{U}}(\mathbf{A}, \mathbf{B})$ thatthat is a formal expression of the assertion that *equivalent types are identical.*

If we think of types as spaces, **U** is a space, the points of which are themselves spaces. $\mathbf{Id}_{\mathrm{U}}(\mathbf{A}, \mathbf{B})$ is also a space, whose points are paths p: $\mathbf{A} \rightsquigarrow \mathbf{B}$ in **U**. The Univalence Principle asserts that in a certain sense, the points of $\mathbf{Id}_{\mathrm{U}}(\mathbf{A}, \mathbf{B})$ are correlated exactly with homotopy equivalences $\mathbf{A} \simeq \mathbf{B}$.

Thus, for small types **A** and **B**, that is, points of the universe **U**, the Univalence Principle identifies the following three notions, which are *logical, topological*, and *homotopical*, respectively,

- an identification $p{:}\mathbf{A} = \mathbf{B}$ of **A** and **B**,
- a path p: $\mathbf{A} \rightsquigarrow \mathbf{B}$ from **A** to **B** in **U**, and
- an equivalence $p{:}\mathbf{A} \simeq \mathbf{B}$ between **A** and **B.**

The Univalence Principle may be put punningly,
Identity is equivalent to equivalence
or, metaphorically,
Equivalent types are equal.

The Univalence Principle can be regarded as a principle of *extensionality.* Formally, it resembles the Axiom of Extensionality of set theory that asserts

[79] Coquand (2018) and Escardo (2018).

[80] The argument here, which is non-trivial, is presented in full in Escardo (2018) and Homotopy (2013).

that any two sets equivalent in the sense of having the same elements are identical. Surprisingly, it implies[81] the principle of *function extensionality* that any two point-wise equal functions are identical.

Homotopy Type Theory with the Univalence Principle is sometimes called *univalent foundations* or *univalent mathematics*.[82]

Sets in Univalent Foundations give rise to a category **USet** with objects all sets and arrows all functions between them. Under the assumption that there is a type of all propositions, it can be shown[83] that **USet** is a topos. Since toposes are 'generalized categories of sets', this provides a strong sense in which Univalent Foundations can be regarded as an extension of set theory.

In classical mathematics, isomorphic mathematical entities are often said to have an 'identical structure', although the objects themselves, considered as sets, may be quite different. For example, the additive group **Z** of the integers and the additive group **2Z** of the even integers are different as sets but isomorphic as groups and so have an 'identical structure'. Now, the Univalence Principle implies the startling assertion that isomorphic mathematical entities do not merely have 'identical structure' but *are themselves identical.* We might call this *Isomorphism is Identity Principle.* Thus, the Univalence Principle may be seen as amounting to an *enlargement* of the notion of identity so that it coincides with isomorphism. Another way of looking at it is that the effect of the Univalence Principle is to restrict the notion of *property* to what may be termed *structural, or formal* properties, namely, properties P that are preserved under isomorphism in the sense of satisfying the condition, for structures $\mathfrak{A}$, $\mathfrak{B}$,

$\mathfrak{A} \cong \mathfrak{B}$ and $P(\mathfrak{A}) \Rightarrow P(\mathfrak{B})$.[84]

It is a common view among mathematicians that structural properties are the truly fundamental properties of mathematical entities, and the incidental contentual features that they happen to acquire through their manner of construction – usually within set theory – are extraneous from a strictly mathematical point of view. That is, in mathematics, what counts in the end is *form*, rather than *content.* Univalent Foundations provides a striking embodiment of

[81] Homotopy (2013, section 4.9).

[82] It is natural to ask whether univalent mathematics is *consistent.* Voevodsky has shown that it can be modelled in the category of simplicial sets, thereby showing that it is consistent relative to Zermelo–Fraenkel set theory with two inaccessible cardinals. See Kapulkin and Lumsdaine (2018).

[83] Homotopy (2013, theorem 10.1.12.).

[84] In particular, since an isomorphism of sets is just a bijection, the only properties of sets expressible in Univalent Foundations are those that are preserved under bijections. In Univalent Foundations, sets are essentially just cardinal numbers, purely abstract collections of 'dots'. See Bell (2006).

this idea.[85] Its supporters believe that it offers a new foundation for mathematics in which mathematical objects are characterized entirely by their form as opposed to their content.

It is interesting to note that Voevodsky's original motivation[86] for investigating type theory was very far from the desire to realize the isomorphism is an identity principle, or anything like it. His primary reason was much more down-to-earth. His own experience as a mathematician had led him to worry that mathematical proofs (including his own) were becoming so lengthy and complicated as to bid fair to defy the ability of mathematicians to check them for mistakes.[87] To prevent this from happening, he conceived the idea of constructing a framework for the formalization of mathematics, which could be implemented on a computer in such a way that each step in a formalized proof could be checked automatically by an installed programme – a *proof assistant*. The language of type theory as developed by Martin-Löf and others, with its explicit presentation of rules of procedure, recommended itself as a language in which to set up the framework for the proof assistant Voevodsky sought.[88] Homotopy theory, an area in which Voevodsky was an expert and to which he had made outstanding contributions, provided a fruitful way of interpreting the type-theoretic language. This led to the Univalence Principle and its remarkable consequences.

Voevodsky's worries about mathematical mistakes stimulated the development of Homotopy Type Theory and univalent mathematics. Nearly a century earlier, Russell's worries about mathematical paradoxes led to the invention of type theory. The parallel is striking. If Homotopy Type Theory were to replace set theory as a foundation for mathematics, wouldn't that be Russell's revenge?

[85] For an illuminating discussion, see Escardo (2019).

[86] Voevodsky (2014).

[87] Mathematicians are, perhaps, more than any other professional group, afraid of making mistakes. (Even worse, though, is the fear of having one's fellow practitioners dismissing one's work as 'trivial'.) The so-called 'mathematicians' nightmare' is the fear that the future development of mathematics may come to depend on the acceptance of a theorem whose proof conceals a hidden flaw that never comes to be revealed.

[88] In Voevodsky (2014), we find the remark:

> *And now I do my mathematics with a proof assistant. I have a lot of wishes in terms of getting this proof assistant to work better, but at least I don't have to go home and worry about having made a mistake in my work. I know that if I did something, I did it, and I don't have to come back to it nor do I have to worry about my arguments being too complicated or about how to convince others my arguments are correct. I can just trust the computer.*

Appendix

The Semantics of Local Set Theory/ Intuitionistic Higher-Order Logic

A.1 Categories

The semantics we have sketched for second- and higher-order logical systems, as well as for Church's simple type theory, are each based on set theory. However, the natural semantical framework for local set theories or intuitionistic higher-order logic rests not on set theory as such but on the mathematical discipline called *category theory,* more specifically, on the category-theoretic concept of (elementary) *topos.* A topos may be regarded as the embodiment within category theory of the idea of a higher-order structure. In this Appendix, we sketch the basic concepts of category theory, define the topos concept, and show how these ideas can be used in the formulation of a semantical framework for intuitionistic higher-order logic.

Devised by Eilenberg and Mac Lane[1] in the early 1940s, *category theory* is a presentation of mathematics in terms of the fundamental concepts of *transformation* and *composition* of transformations. While the importance of these concepts had long been recognized in algebra (e.g., by Galois through the idea of a group of permutations) and in geometry (e.g., by Klein in his *Erlangen program*), the truly universal role they play in mathematics did not really begin to be appreciated until the rise of abstract algebra in the 1930s. In abstract algebra, the idea of transformation of structure (homomorphism) was central from the beginning, and it soon became apparent to algebraists that its most important concepts and constructions were in fact formulable in terms of that idea alone. Thus emerged the view that the essence of a mathematical structure is to be sought not in its internal constitution, but rather in the nature of its relationships with other structures of the same kind, as manifested through the network of transformations. This idea has achieved its fullest expression in category theory, an axiomatic framework within which the notions of transformation (as *morphism* or *arrow*) and composition (and also structure, as *object*) are fundamental, that is, *are not defined in terms of anything else.*

[1] Eilenberg and Mac Lane (1945).

What, precisely, is a category? Formally, a *category* **C** is determined by first specifying two collections *Ob*(**C**) and *Arr*(**C**) – the assemblies of **C**-*objects* and **C**-*arrows*, **C**-*morphisms, or* **C**-*maps*. These are subject to the following axioms:

- Each **C**-arrow f is assigned a pair of C-objects dom(f), cod(f) called the *domain* and *codomain* of f, respectively. To indicate the fact that **C**-objects X and Y are, respectively, the domain and codomain of f, we write f: $X \to Y$ or $X \xrightarrow{f} Y$. The collection of **C**-arrows with domain X and codomain Y is written **C**(X, Y).
- Each **C**-object X is assigned a **C**-arrow $1_X: X \to X$ called the *identity arrow* on X.
- Each pair f, g of **C**-arrows such that cod(f) = dom(g) is assigned an arrow $g \circ f$: dom(f) $\to$ cod(g) called the *composite* of f and g. Thus, if f: $X \to Y$ and g: $Y \to Z$, then $g \circ f$: X→Z. We also write $X \xrightarrow{f} Y \xrightarrow{g} Z$ for $g \circ f$. Arrows f, g satisfying cod(f) = dom(g) are called *composable*.
- *Associativity law.* For composable arrows (f, g) and (g, h), we have $h \circ (g \circ f) = h \circ (g \circ f)$.
- *Identity law.* For any arrow f: $X \to Y$, we have $f \circ 1_X = f = 1_Y \circ f$.

An arrow f: $X \to Y$ is *invertible* or an *isomorphism* if there is an arrow g: $Y \to X$ such that $g \circ f = 1_X f \circ g = 1_Y$. Two objects X and Y are *isomorphic,* written $X \cong Y$ if there is an isomorphism between them.

As a basic example of a category, we have the category **Set** of sets whose objects are all sets and whose arrows are all maps between sets (strictly, triples (f, A, B) with domain (f) = A and range (f) $\subseteq B$). Other examples of categories are the category of groups with objects all groups and arrows all group homomorphisms, the category of topological spaces with objects all topological spaces and arrows all continuous maps, and the category of manifolds with objects all differentiable manifolds and arrows all smooth functions between them. Categories with just one object may be identified with *monoids*, that is, algebraic structures with an associative multiplication and an identity element. A category in which every arrow is invertible is called a *groupoid;* groupoids with one element may be identified with *groups*. The most important example of a groupoid is the *fundamental groupoid* of a topological space X, in which the objects are the points of X and an arrow from a point a to a point b is an equivalence class of paths from a to b, where two paths are equivalent if they are homotopic.

In many instances, a category may be thought of as an explicit presentation of a *mathematical form or concept*. In these cases, the objects of the category may be considered as the *instances* of the associated form and the morphisms or arrows are the transformations between these instances, which in some specified sense 'preserve' this form. As examples, we have:

Category	***Form***	***Transformation***
Sets	Pure discreteness	Functional correlations
Groups	Composition/inversion	Homomorphisms
Topological spaces	Continuity	Continuous maps
Differentiable manifolds	Smoothness	Smooth maps

A.2 Basic Category-Theoretic Definitions

We tabulate some fundamental category-theoretic definitions.

Commutative diagram (in category)	Diagram of objects and arrows such that the arrow obtained by composing the arrows of any connected path depends only on the endpoints of the path
Initial object	Object 0 such that for any object X, there is a unique arrow $0 \to X$(e.g., $\varnothing$ in **Set**)
Terminal object	Object 1 such that for any object X, there is a unique arrow $X \to 1$(e.g., any singleton in **Set**)
Element of an object X	Arrow $1 \to X$
Monic arrow $X \rightarrowtail Y$	Arrow f: $X \to Y$ such that for any arrows g, h: $Z \to X$, $f \circ g = f \circ h \Rightarrow g = h$ (in **Set,** *one-one* map)
Epic arrow $X \twoheadrightarrow Y$	Arrow f: $X \to Y$ such that for any arrows g, h: $Z \to X$, $g \circ f = h \circ f \Rightarrow g = h$ (in **Set,** *onto* map)
Product of objects X, Y	Object $X \times Y$ with arrows (projections) $X \xleftarrow{\pi_1} X \times Y \xrightarrow{\pi_2} Y$ such that any diagram 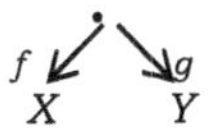 can be uniquely completed to a commutative diagram 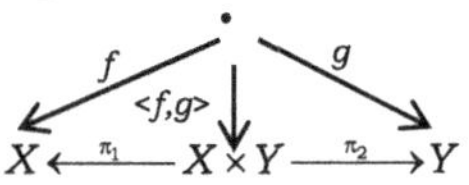
Product of arrows f_1: $X_1 \to Y_1$, f_2: $X_2 \to Y_2$	Unique arrow $f_1 \times f_2$: $X_1 \times X_2 \to Y_1 \times Y_2$ making the diagram

(cont.)

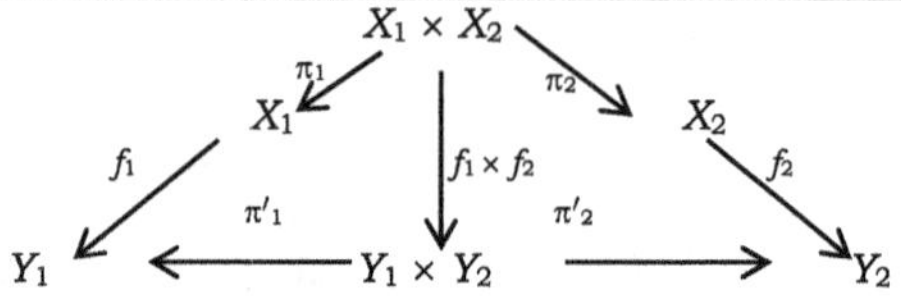

commute. That is, $f_1 \times f_2 = <f_1 \circ \pi_1, f_2 \circ \pi_2>$.

Diagonal arrow on object X — Unique arrow $\delta_X : X \to X \times X$ making the diagram

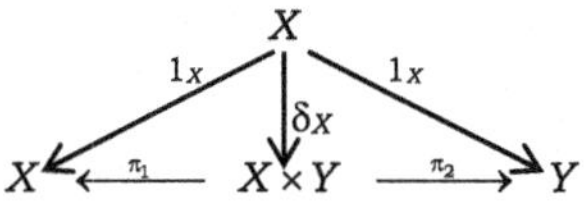

commute. That is, $\delta_X = <1_X,\ 1_X>$.

Coproduct of objects X, Y — Object $X + Y$ together with a pair of arrows $X \xrightarrow{\sigma_1} X + Y \xleftarrow{\sigma_2} Y$ such that for any pair of arrows $X \xrightarrow{f} A \xleftarrow{g} B$, there is a unique arrow $X + Y \xrightarrow{h} A$ such that the diagram

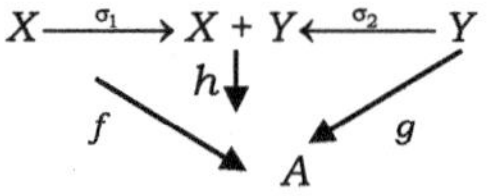

commutes.

Pullback diagram or *square* — Commutative diagram of the form

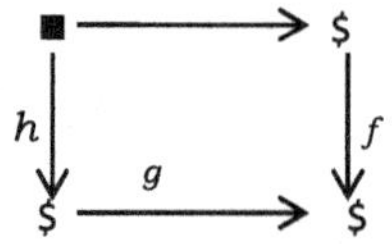

such that for any commutative diagram

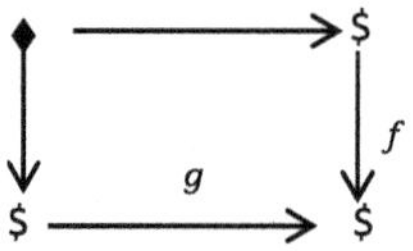

there is a unique arrow ♦ $\xrightarrow{!}$ ■ making the diagram

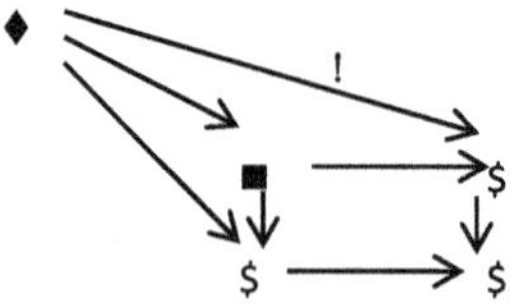

commute.

h is called the *pullback* of g (along f)

Equalizer of pair of arrows $\$ \overset{f}{\underset{g}{\rightrightarrows}} \blacksquare$ — Arrow $\blacklozenge \xrightarrow{e} \$$ such that $f \circ e = g \circ e$ and, for any arrow $\blacktriangle \xrightarrow{e'} \$$ such that $f \circ e' = g \circ e'$ there is a unique $\blacktriangle \xrightarrow{u} \blacklozenge$ making the diagram

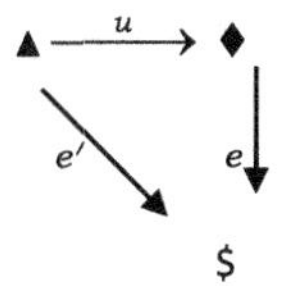

commute

Subobject of an object X — Pair (m, Y), with m a monic arrow $Y \rightarrowtail X$

Inclusion of subobjects — For $m : Y \rightarrowtail X$, $n : Z \rightarrowtail X$, $m \subseteq n$ if there is $f: Y \rightarrow Z$ such that $n \circ f = m$

Truth value object or *subobject classifier* — Object Ω together with arrow $t : 1 \rightarrow \Omega$ such that every monic m: $\$ \rightarrowtail \blacklozenge$ (i.e., subobject of $\blacklozenge$) can be uniquely extended to a pullback diagram of the form

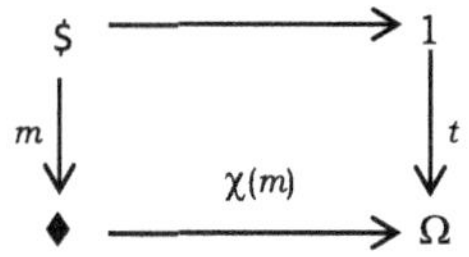

$\chi(m)$ is the *characteristic arrow* of m.

Conversely, any diagram of the form $\blacklozenge \xrightarrow{u} \Omega \xleftarrow{t} 1$ must have a pullback. The pullback of u will be written $\bar{u}$. It is necessarily monic.

The next few definitions assume that the ambient category has a terminal object, products, and a subobject classifier. It can be shown that in any such category, every monic arrow has a pullback.

Partial ordering ≤ on arrows to Ω — For $u,v: A\to\Omega$, $u\leq v$ iff $\overline{u}\subseteq\overline{v}$

Intersection of subobjects — For monics m and n with common codomain
A, form the pullback square

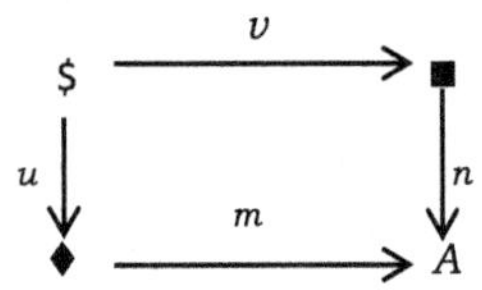

The map $m\circ u(=n\circ v)$ is the intersection $m\cap n$ of m and n.

Meet of two maps to Ω — For $u\ v: A\to\Omega$, $u\wedge v=\chi(\overline{u}\cap\overline{v})$

Equality arrow $A\times A\to\Omega$ — $eq_A=\chi(\delta_A)$

Power object of an object X — An object PX together
with an arrow ('evaluation')
$e_X: X\times PX\to\Omega$ such that
for any $f: X\times PX\to\Omega$, there is a unique arrow $f: Y\to PX$ such that
the diagram

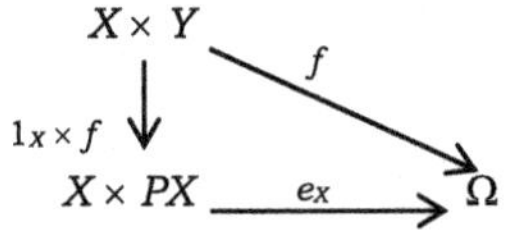

commutes. (In **Set**, PX is the power set of X, and e_X is the characteristic function of the membership relation between X and PX.)

Exponential object of objects Y and X — An object Y^X, together with an arrow $ev: XX\times Y^X\to Y$ such that for any arrow $f: X\times Z\to Y$, there is a unique arrow $f: Z\to Y^X$ -the *exponential transpose* of f– making the diagram

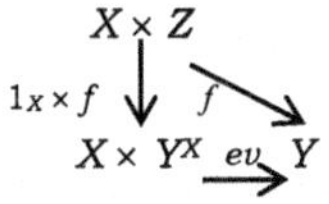

commute. In Set, Y^X is the set of all maps $X\to Y$ and ev is the map that sends (x, f) to $f(x)$.

A *functor* F: C→D between two categories **C** and D is a map that 'preserves commutative diagrams', that is, assigns to each C-object A a D-object FA and to each C-arrow f: $A \to B$ a D-arrow Ff: $FA \to FB$ in such a way that:

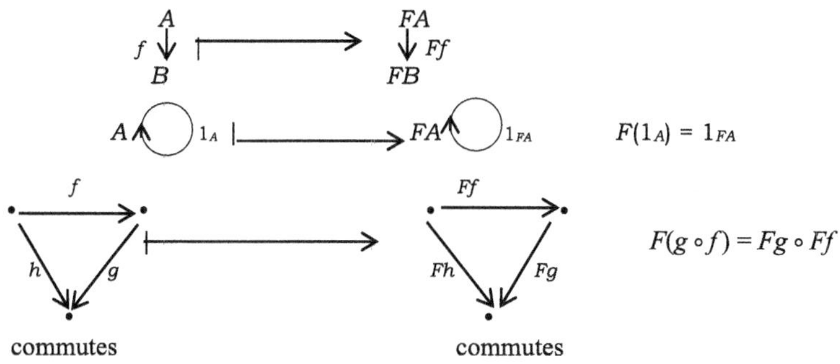

A functor F: **C**→**D** is an *equivalence* if it is 'an isomorphism up to isomorphism', that is, if it is

- *faithful:* $Ff = Fg \Rightarrow f = g$,
- *full*: for any h: $FA \to FB$ there is f: $A \to B$ such that $h = Ff$, and
- *dense:* for any **D**-object B there is a **C**-object A such that $B \cong FA$.

Two categories are *equivalent,* written $\cong$, if there is an equivalence between them. Equivalence is the appropriate notion of *identity of form* for categories.

A category is *cartesian closed* if it has a terminal object, as well as products and exponentials of arbitrary pairs of its objects. It is *finitely complete* if it has a terminal object, products of arbitrary pairs of its objects, and equalizers. A(n) (elementary) *topos* is a category possessing a terminal object, products, a truth-value object, and power objects. It can be shown that every topos is cartesian closed and finitely complete (so that this notion of topos is equivalent to that originally given by Lawvere and Tierney). The category **Set** is a topos. For our purposes, a topos may think of as 'generalized category of sets'.

A.3 Topos Semantics for Local Set Theory: The Soundness, Completeness and Equivalence Theorems

We next describe *topos semantics* for local set theory. This is based on the idea of an *interpretation* of a local language in a topos.

Let $\mathscr{L}$ be a local language and **E** a topos. An *interpretation* I of $\mathscr{L}$ in **E** is an assignment:

- to each type **A**, of an **E**-object $\mathbf{A}_I$ such that:

  $(\mathbf{A}_1 \times \ldots \times \mathbf{A}_n)_I = (\mathbf{A}_1)_I \times \ldots \times (\mathbf{A}_n)_I$

  $(\mathbf{PA})_I = P\mathbf{A}_I$,

  $\mathbf{1}_I = 1$, the terminal object of **E,**

  $\mathbf{\Omega}_I = \Omega$, the truth-value object of **E**.
- to each function symbol **f**: $\mathbf{A} \to \mathbf{B}$, an **E**-arrow $f_I : \mathbf{A}_I \to \mathbf{B}_I$.

We shall sometimes write A_{E} or just A for $\mathbf{A}_I$.

We extend I to terms of $\mathcal{L}$ as follows. If τ **: B**, write $\boldsymbol{x}$ for $(x_1, \ldots, x_n)$ any sequence of variables containing all variables of τ (and call such sequences *adequate* for τ). Define the **E**-arrow

$$[\![\tau]\!]_x : A_1 \times \ldots \times A_n \to B$$

recursively as follows:

$$[\![\star]\!]_x : A_1 \times \ldots \times A_n \to 1,$$

$$[\![x_i]\!]_x = \pi_i : A_1 \times \ldots \times A_n \to A_i,$$

$$[\![\mathbf{f}(\tau)]\!]_x = f_I \circ [\![\tau]\!]_x,$$

$$[\![< \tau_1, \ldots, \tau_n >]\!]_x = < [\![\tau_1]\!]_x, \ldots, [\![\tau_n]\!]_x >,$$

$$[\![(\tau)_i]\!]_x = \pi_i \circ [\![\tau_x]\!],$$

$$[\![\{y : \alpha\}]\!]_x = \left([\![\alpha(y/u)]\!]_{ux} \circ can \right)^{\wedge},$$

where, in this last clause, u differs from $x_1, \ldots$, *xn and* is free for y in α, y is of type **C** (so that B is of type **PC**), *can* is the canonical isomorphism $C \times (A_1 \times \ldots \times A_n) \cong C \times A_1 \times \ldots \times A_n$, and f is as defined for power objects. To understand why, consider the diagrams

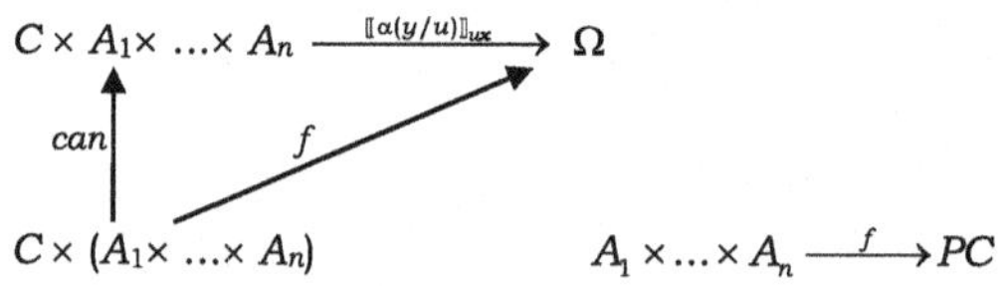

$$A_1 \times \ldots \times A_n \xrightarrow{f} PC.$$

In set theory, $f(a_1, \ldots, a_n) = \{y \in C : \alpha(y, a_1, \ldots, a_n)\}$, so we take $[\![\{y : \alpha\}]\!]_x$ to be f.

Finally,

$[\![\sigma = \tau]\!]_x = eq_C \circ [\![< \sigma, \tau >]\!]_x$ (with σ, τ : **C**),
$[\![\sigma \in \tau]\!]_x = e_C \circ [\![< \sigma, \tau >]\!]_x$ (with σ : **C**, τ : **PC** and where eC is as defined for power objects).

If τ : **B** is closed, then $\boldsymbol{x}$ may be taken to be the empty sequence $\varnothing$. In this case, we write $[\![\tau]\!]$ for $[\![\tau]\!]\,\varnothing$; this is an arrow $1 \rightarrow B$.

We note that

$$[\![\mathsf{T}]\!]_x = [\![\star = \star]\!]_x = eq \circ < [\![\star]\!]_x, [\![\star]\!]_x >= T.$$

For any finite set $\Gamma = \{\alpha_1, \ldots, \alpha_m\}$ of formulas, write

$[\![\Gamma]\!]_{I,x}$ for $[\![\alpha_I]\!]_{I,x} \wedge \ldots \wedge [\![\alpha_m]\!]_{I,x}$ if $m \geq 1$ or T if $\mathrm{m} = 0$.

Given a formula α, let $\boldsymbol{x} = (x_1, \ldots, x_n)$ list all the free variables in $\Gamma \cup \{\alpha\}$; write

$\Gamma \vDash_I \alpha$ for $[\![\Gamma]\!]_{I,x} \leq [\![\alpha]\!]_{I,x}$.

$\Gamma \vDash_I \alpha$ is read : 'Γ : α is *valid* under the interpretation I in **E**'. If S is a local set theory, we say that I is a *model* of S if every sequent of S is valid under I. Notice that

$\vDash_I \beta$ iff $[\![\beta]\!]_x = T$.

So if I is an interpretation in a *degenerate* topos, that is, a topos possessing just one object up to isomorphism, then $\vDash_I \alpha$ for all α.

We write

$\Gamma \vDash \alpha$ for $\vDash_I \alpha$ for every I and
$\Gamma \vDash_S \alpha$ for $\Gamma \vDash_I \alpha$ for every model I of S.

It can be shown (laboriously) that the basic axioms and rules of inference of any local set theory are valid under every interpretation. This yields the

Soundness Theorem for Local Set Theory

$$\Gamma \vdash \alpha \Rightarrow \Gamma \vDash \alpha \quad \Gamma \vdash_s \alpha \Rightarrow \Gamma \vDash_s \alpha.$$

A local set theory S is said to be *consistent* if it is not the case that $\vdash_S \bot$. The soundness theorem yields the

Corollary. *Any pure local set theory is consistent.*

Proof. Set up an interpretation I of $\mathcal{L}$ in the topos **Finset** of finite sets as follows: $\mathbf{1}_I = 1, \mathbf{\Omega}_I = \{0, 1\} = 2$; for any ground type $\mathbf{A}$, $\mathbf{A}_I$ is any non-empty finite set. Extend I to arbitrary types in an obvious way. Finally, $\mathbf{f}_I : \mathbf{A}_I \to \mathbf{B}_I$ is to be any map from $\mathbf{A}_I$ to $\mathbf{B}_I$.

If $\vdash \bot$, then $\vdash \alpha$, so $\vDash_I \alpha$ for any formula α. In particular $\vDash_I u = v$, where u and v are variables of type **P1.** Hence, $[\![u]\!]_{I,uv} = [\![v]\!]_{I,uv}$, that is, the two projections $P1 \times P1 \to P1$ would have to be identical, a contradiction.

Given a local set theory S, recall that in Section 3.2, we introduced the category of S-sets $\mathbf{C}(S)$. Then $\mathbf{C}(S)$ is a topos.

The terminal object of $\mathbf{C}(S)$ is $U\mathbf{1}$; the product of two objects (S-sets) X and Y is the S-set $X \times Y$, with projections given by

$$\pi_1 = (<x,y> \mapsto x) : X \times Y \to X,$$
$$\pi_2 = (<x,y> \mapsto x) : X \times Y \to Y;$$

its truth-value object is (Ω, t), where $t : 1 \to \Omega$ is the S-map $\{<\star, \mathrm{T}>\}$, and the power object of an object X is (PX, e_X), where $e_X : X \times PX \to \Omega$ is the S-map $<x, z> \mapsto x \in z$. All this is proved in much the same way as for classical set theory.

Given a local set theory S in a language $\mathcal{L}$, we define the *canonical interpretation* $C(S)$ of $\mathcal{L}$ in $\mathbf{C}(S)$ by:

$$\mathbf{A}_{C(S)} = U_{\mathbf{A}} \quad \mathbf{f}_{C(S)} = (x \mapsto \mathbf{f}(x)) : U_{\mathbf{A}} \to U_{\mathbf{B}} \text{ for } \mathbf{f} : \mathbf{A} \to \mathbf{B}$$

A straightforward induction establishes

$$[\![\tau]\!]_{C(S),x} = (x \mapsto \tau).$$

This yields

$$(*) \quad \Gamma \vDash_{C(S)} \alpha \Leftrightarrow \Gamma \vdash_S \alpha.$$

For:

$$\begin{aligned} \vDash_{C(s)} \alpha &\Leftrightarrow [\![\alpha]\!]_{C(S)_x} = T \\ &\Leftrightarrow (x \mapsto \alpha) = (x \mapsto \mathrm{T}) \\ &\Leftrightarrow \vdash_S \alpha = \mathrm{T} \\ &\Leftrightarrow \vdash_S \alpha. \end{aligned}$$

Since $\Gamma \vdash_S \alpha \Leftrightarrow \vdash_S \gamma \to \alpha$, where γ is the conjunction of all the formulas in Γ, the special case yields the general one.

Equivalence (*) asserts that the sequents valid under the canonical interpretation $C(S)$ are *precisely* the sequents of S. We express this by saying that $C(S)$ is a *canonical model* of S.

This fact yields the

Completeness Theorem for Local Set Theory

$$\Gamma \vDash \alpha \Leftrightarrow \Gamma \vdash \alpha \qquad \Gamma \vDash_S \alpha \Leftrightarrow \Gamma \vdash_s \alpha.$$

Proof. We know that $C(S)$ is a model of S. Therefore, using (*),

$$\Gamma \vDash_S \alpha \Rightarrow \Gamma \vdash_{C(s)} \alpha \Rightarrow \Gamma \vdash_S \alpha.$$

The result now follows from the soundness theorem.

The completeness theorem for local set theories is a precise analogy, based on topos semantics, of the completeness theorems for first- and higher-order logic.

We have shown that each local set theory S determines a topos **C**(S) and an interpretation in that topos making it a model of S. Inversely, given an arbitrary topos **E**, we can construct a local set theory $Th(\mathbf{E})$ within a local language $\mathscr{L}_{\mathrm{E}}$, along with an interpretation of $\mathscr{L}_{\mathrm{E}}$ in **E,** whose valid sequents coincide with the sequents in $Th(\mathbf{E})$.

We define the local language $\mathscr{L}_{\mathrm{E}}$ determined by **E** – the *internal language* of **E** – as follows. The ground type symbols of $\mathscr{L}_{\mathrm{E}}$ are taken to match the objects of **E** other than its terminal and truth-value objects, that is, for each **E**-object A (other than 1, Ω) we assume given a ground type **A** in $\mathscr{L}_{\mathrm{E}}$. Next, we define for each type symbol **A** an **E**-object $\mathbf{A_E}$ by

$$\mathbf{A_E} = \mathbf{A} \text{ for ground types } \mathbf{A},$$

$$(\mathbf{A}\times\mathbf{B})_{\mathrm{E}} = \mathbf{A_E}\times\mathbf{B}_{\mathrm{E}}^{2}$$

$$(\mathbf{PA})_{\mathrm{E}} = P(\mathbf{A})_{\mathrm{E}}.$$

The function symbols of $\mathscr{L}_{\mathrm{E}}$ are triples $(f, \mathbf{A}, \mathbf{B}) = f$ with f: $\mathbf{A}_{\mathrm{E}} \rightarrow \mathbf{B}_{\mathrm{E}}$ in **E**. The signature of ***f*** is **A**→B.[3]

The *natural interpretation* – denoted by E – of $\mathscr{L}_{\mathbf{E}}$ in **E** is determined by the assignments

[2] Note that if we write C for $A \times B$, while **C** is a ground type, then A × B is a product type. Nevertheless, $\mathbf{C}_E = (\mathbf{A} \times \mathrm{B})_E$.

[3] Note the following: if $f : A \times B \rightarrow D$, in **E**, then writing C for $A \times B$ as in the footnote above, (f, **C**, **D**) and (f, **A** × **B**, **D**) are both function symbols of $\mathscr{L}_{\mathrm{E}}$**E** associated with f. But the former has signature **C**→**D**, while the latter has the different signature **A** × **B**→**D**..

$\mathbf{A}_E = \mathbf{A}$ for each ground type $\mathbf{A}$ $\quad (f, \mathbf{A}, \mathbf{B})_E = f$.

The local set theory *Th*(**E**), the *theory* (or *internal logic*) of **E,** is the theory in $\mathcal{L}_\mathrm{E}$ generated by the collection of all sequents $\Gamma : \alpha$ such that $\Gamma \vDash_E \alpha$ under the natural interpretation E of $\mathcal{L}_\mathbf{E}$ in **E**. Then we have

$$\Gamma \vdash_{Th(\mathbf{E})} \alpha \Leftrightarrow \Gamma \vDash_E \alpha.$$

If $\Gamma \vdash_{Th(\mathbf{E})\alpha}$ then by the soundness theorem $\Gamma \vdash_{Th(\mathbf{E})\alpha} \alpha$ i.e., $\Gamma : \alpha$ is valid in every model of *Th*(**E**).

But, by definition, E is a model of *Th*(**E**) so that $\Gamma : \alpha$ is valid under E. The converse holds by definition of *Th*(**E**)**.**

It can be further shown (although we shall not give the proof here) that the natural functor $F : \mathbf{E} \to \mathbf{C}(\mathrm{Th}(\mathbf{E}))$ defined by

$FA = U_\mathbf{A}$ for each **E**-object A
$Ff = (x \mapsto f(x)) : U_\mathbf{A} \to U_\mathbf{B}$ for each **E**-arrow $f : A \to B$

is an e*quivalence of categories*. This has the following important consequence. Call any topos of the form *Th*(**E**) *linguistic.* Then any topos is equivalent to a linguistic topos. This is known as the *equivalence theorem.*

To sum up. Each local set theory *S* determines a topos, the *canonical model* of *S.* Inversely, each topos **E** determines a local set theory whose canonical model is equivalent to **E.** Thus, in a certain sense, the *syntax and semantics of local set theory/intuitionistic higher-order logic are equivalent.* This is a unique feature not shared by other forms of type theory.

Bibliography

Aczel, P. (1978). The type-theoretic interpretation of constructive set theory. In A. ManIntyre, L. Pacholski, and J. Paris, eds., *Logic Colloquium 77*, pp. 55–66. North-Holland.

(1982). The type-theoretic interpretation of constructive set theory: Choice principles. In A. S. Troelstra and D. van Dalen, eds., *The L.E.J. Brouwer Centenary Symposium*, pp. 1–40. North- Holland.

(1986). The type-theoretic interpretation of constructive set theory: Inductive definitions. In R. Barcan Marcus, G. J. W. Dorn, and P. Weinegartner, eds., *Logic, Methodology and Philosophy of Science VII*, pp. 17–49. North-Holland.

and Gambino, N. (2002). Collection principles in dependent type theory. In P. Callaghan, Z. Luo, J. McKinna, and R. Pollack, eds., *Types for Proofs and Programs,* Volume 2277 of *Lecture Notes on Computer Science*, pp. 1–23. Springer.

(2005). The generalized type-theoretic interpretation of constructive set theory. Manuscript available on first author's webpage www.cs.man.ac.uk/~petera/papers

and Rathjen, M. (2001). Notes on Constructive Set Theory. Technical Report 40, Mittag-Leffler Institute, The Swedish Royal Academy of Sciences. Available on first author's webpage www.cs.man.ac.uk/~petera/papers

Awodey, S. (2017). Structuralism, invariance, and univalence. In Landry (2017), pp. 58–68.

and Warren, M. A. (2009). Homotopy theoretic models of identity types. *Math. Proc. Cambridge Philos. Soc.* **146(1)**, 45–55.

Barendregt, H. (1984). *The Lambda Calculus, Its Syntax and Semantics*. Studies in Logic and the Foundations of Mathematics, Volume 103. North-Holland.

(1992). *Lambda Calculi with Types*. Handbook of Logic in Computer Science, Volume 2. Oxford University Press, pp. 117–309.

Bell, J. L. (1988). *Toposes and Local Set Theories: An Introduction*. Oxford Logic Guides, Volume 14. Clarendon Press. Reprinted by Dover (2008).

(2006). Absolute and variable sets in category theory. In G. Sica, ed., *What Is Category Theory?*, pp. 9-17. Polimetrica. https://publish.uwo.ca/~jbell/catset.pdf

(2012). Types, sets and categories. In A. Kanamori, D. Gabbay, and J. Woods, eds., *Sets and Extensions in the 20th Century*. Handbook of the History of Logic, Volume 6, pp. 633–88. Elsevier.

and Machover, M. (1977). *A Course in Mathematic al Logic*. Elsevier.

Benzmüller, C., and Andrews, P. B. (2019). Church's type theory. *Stanford Encyclopedia of Philosophy*. https://plato.stanford.edu/entries/type-theory-church/

Bishop, E. (1967). *Foundations of Constructive Analysis*. McGraw-Hill.

Boileau, A. (1975). *Types vs. Topos*. Thesis, Univesité de Montreal.

and Joyal, A. (1981). La logique de topos. *J. Symbolic Logic* **46**, 6–16.

Boolos, G. (1997). Constructing Cantorian counterexamples. *J. Phil. Logic* **26**, 237–39.

Carnap, R. (1929). *Abriss der Logistik*. Springer.

Church, A. (1940). A formulation of the simple theory of types. *J. Symbolic Logic* **1**, 56–68.

(1976). Comparison of Russell's resolution of the semantical antinomies with that of Tarski. *J. Symbolic Logic* **41**, 747–60.

Chwistek, L. (1925). Theory of constructive types. *Annales de la soc. Pol. De Math.* **3**, 92–141.

Coquand, T. (2018). Type theory. *Stanford Encyclopedia of Philosophy*. https://plato.stanford.edu/entries/type-theory/

and Huet, G. (1988). The calculus of constructions. *Inf. and Comp.* **76(2/3)**, 95–120.

Crole, R. (1993). *Categories for Types*. Cambridge University Press.

Curry, H. B., and Feys, R. (1958). *Combinatory Logic*. North-Holland.

Diaconescu, R. (1975). Axiom of choice and complementation. *Proc. Amer. Math. Soc.* **51**, 176–78.

Eilenberg, S., and Mac Lane, S. (1945). General theory of natural equivalences. *Trans. Amer. Math. Soc.* **58**, 231–94.

(1986). *Eilenberg-Mac Lane: Collected Works*. Academic Press.

Escardo, M. (2018). A self-contained, brief and complete formulation of Voevodsky's Univalence Axiom. 1803.02294.pdf (arxiv.org) https://arxiv.org/abs/1803.02294

(2019). Equality of mathematical structures. pdf(arxiv.org). www.cs.bham.ac.uk/~mhe/.talks/xii-pcc.pdf#page1

Farmer, W. (2006). The seven virtues of simple type theory. imps.mcmaster.ca/doc/seven-virtues.pdf

Fourman, M. P. (1974). *Connections between Category Theory and Logic*. D. Phil. Thesis, Oxford University.

(1977). The logic of topoi. In J. Barwise, ed., *Handbook of Mathematical Logic*, pp. 1053–90. North-Holland.

Mulvey, C. J., and Scott, D. S., eds. (1979). *Applications of Sheaves. Proceedings. L.M.S. Durham Symposium* 1977. Springer Lecture Notes in Mathematics, Volume 753.

Frege, G. (1879) *Begriffsschrift, eine der arithmetischen nachgebildete Formelsprache des reinen Denkens*, Halle a. S.: Louis Nebert (translated as *Concept Script, a formal language of pure thought modelled upon that of arithmetic*, by S. Bauer-Mengelberg). In J. van Heijenoort, ed., *From Frege to Gödel: A Source Book in Mathematical Logic, 1879–1931*. Harvard University Press, 1967.

Gandy, R. O. (1977). The simple theory of types. In R. Gandy and M. Hyland, eds., *Logic Colloquium 76*, pp. 173–81. North-Holland.

Girard, J.-Y. (1972). *Interprétation fonctionelle élimination des coupures dans l'arithmétique d'ordre supérieure*. Ph.D. Thesis, Université Paris VII.

Gödel, K. (1931). Über formal untenscheidbare Sätze der Principia Mathematica und verwandter Systeme I. *Monatsh. Math. Phys*. **38**, 349–60. Reprinted in English translation by S. Feferman et al., eds. as *Godel, Collected Works, Volume 1*, Oxford University Press, 1986.

Goodman, N., and Myhill, J. (1978). Choice implies excluded middle. *Z. Math Logik Grundlag. Math*. **24(5)**, 461.

Henkin, L. (1950). Completeness in the theory of types. *J. Symbolic Logic* **15**, 81–91.

(1963). A theory of propositional types. *Fund. Math*. **52**, 323–44.

Homotopy. (2013). *Homotopy Type Theory: Univalent Foundations of Mathematics*. The Univalent Foundations Program, Institute for Advanced Study.

Howard, W. A. (1980). The formulae-as-types notion of construction. In J. R. Hindley and J. P. Seldin, eds., *To H. B. Curry: Essays on Combinatorial Logic. Lambda Calculus and Formalism*, pp. 479–90. Academic Press.

Jacobs, B. (1999). *Categorical Logic and Type Theory*. Elsevier.

Johnstone, P. T. (1977). *Topos Theory*. Academic Press.

(2002). *Sketches of an Elephant: A Topos Theory Compendium, Volumes 1 and 2*. Oxford Logic Guides Volumes 43 and 44. Clarendon Press.

Kapulkin, K., and Lumsdaine, P. (2018). The simplicial model of univalent foundations (after Voevodsky). https://arxiv.org/pdf/1211.2851.pdf

Lambek, J., and Scott, P. J. (1986). *Introduction to Higher-Order Categorical Logic*. Cambridge University Press.

Landry, E., ed. (2017). *Categories for the Working Philosopher*. Oxford University Press.

Lawvere, F. W. (1971). Quantifiers and sheaves. In *Actes du Congrés Intern. Des Math. Nice 1970*, tome I. pp. 329–34. Paris: Gauthier-Villars.

(1972). Introduction to *Toposes, Algebraic Geometry and Logic*. Springer Lecture Notes in Mathematics, Volume 274, pp. 1–12.

Lewis, C. I. (1918). *A Survey of Symbolic Logic*, 2nd ed. University of California Press. Reprinted by Dover (1960).

Maietti, M. E. (2005). Modular correspondence between dependent type theories and categories including pretopoi and topoi. *Math. Struct. Comp. Sci.* **15(6)**, 1089–145.

and Valentini, S. (1999). Can you add power-sets to Martin-Löf's intuitionistic set theory? *Math. Logic Quarterly* **45**, 521–32.

Martin-Löf, P. (1975). An intuitionistic theory of types; predicative part. In H. E. Rose and J. C. Shepherdson, eds., *Logic Colloquium 73*, pp. 73–118. North-Holland.

(1982). Constructive mathematics and computer programming. In L. C. Cohen, J. Los, H. Pfeiffer, and K. P. Podewski, eds., *Logic, Methodology and Philosophy of Science VI*, pp. 153–79. North-Holland.

(1984). *Intuitionistic Type Theory.* Bibliopolis.

Miquel, A. (2001). A strongly normalising Curry-Howard correspondence for IZF set theory. In *Computer Science Logic*, Lecture Notes in Computer Science, Volume 2803, pp. 441–54. Springer.

Nordström, B., Petersson, K., and Smith, J. M. (1990). *Programming in Martin-Löf's Type Theory.* Oxford University Press.

Ramsey, F. P. (1926). The foundations of mathematics. *Proc. Lond. Math. Soc.* **25**, 338–84.

Russell, B. (1903). *The Principles of Mathematics*. Cambridge University Press.

(1908). Mathematical logic as based on the theory of types. *Am. J. Math.* **30**, 222–62. Reprinted as pp.150–82 in van Heijenoort, ed. (1967).

and Whitehead, A. N. (1910–1913). *Principia Mathematica*, 3 Volumes. Cambridge University Press.

Shulman, M. (2017). *Homotopy Type Theory: A Synthetic Approach to Higher Equalities*. In Landry, E. (2017), pp. 36–57. Oxford University Press.

Tait, W. W. (1994). The law of excluded middle and the axiom of choice. In A. George, ed., *Mathematics and Mind*, pp. 45–70. Oxford University Press.

Tarski, A. (1931). Sur les ensembles definissable de nombres réels I. *Fund. Math.* **17**, 210–29.

Van Dalen, D. (1994). *Logic and Structure*. Springer-Verlag.

van Heijenoort, J., ed. (1967). *From Frege to Gödel: A Source Book in Mathematical Logic, 1879–1931*. Harvard University Press.

Voevodsky, V. (2010). The equivalence axiom and univalent models of type theory. *arXiv. 1402.5556, Bibcode:2014arXiv1402.5556 V*

(2014). The origins and motivations of univalent foundations: A personal mission to develop computer proof verification to avoid mathematical mistakes. www.ias.edu/ideas/2014/voevodsky-origins

(2015). An experimental library of formalized mathematics based on univalent foundations. In *Mathematical Structures in Computer Science*, 25: 1278–1294, Cambridge University Press. http://doi.org/10.1017/S0960129514000577

Weyl, H. (1918). *Das Kontinuum*. Veit. English translation by S. Pollard and T. Bole as *The Continuum: A Critical Examination of the Foundation of Analysis*, Kirksville, Missouri, Thomas Jefferson University Press, 1987.

(1946). Mathematics and logic. A brief survey serving as a preface to a review of 'The Philosophy of Bertrand Russell'. *Am. Math. Monthly* **53**, 2–13.

Zangwill, J. (1977). *Local Set Theory and Topoi*. M.Sc. Thesis, Bristol University.

Zermelo, E. (1908). Untersuchungen über die Grundlagen der Mengenlehre I. *Matematische Annalen* **59**, 261–81. Reprinted as pp. 199–215 of van Heijenoort, ed. (1967).

Acknowledgements

I am grateful to Martin Escardo for his lucid unravellings of certain knotty points – knotty to me, at any rate – in Homotopy Type Theory. Thanks also to the anonymous referees for their helpful comments.

Portions of this Element have been reprinted from the article Bell (2012), with the permission of the publisher, Elsevier.

Cambridge Elements

Philosophy and Logic

Bradley Armour-Garb

SUNY Albany

Brad Armour-Garb is chair and Professor of Philosophy at SUNY Albany. His books include *The Law of Non-Contradiction* (co-edited with Graham Priest and J. C. Beall, 2004), *Deflationary Truth* and *Deflationism and Paradox* (both co-edited with J. C. Beall, 2005), *Pretense and Pathology* (with James Woodbridge, Cambridge University Press, 2015), *Reflections on the Liar* (2017), and *Fictionalism in Philosophy* (co-edited with Fred Kroon, 2020).

Frederick Kroon

The University of Auckland

Frederick Kroon is Emeritus Professor of Philosophy at the University of Auckland. He has authored numerous papers in formal and philosophical logic, ethics, philosophy of language, and metaphysics, and is the author of *A Critical Introduction to Fictionalism* (with Stuart Brock and Jonathan McKeown-Green, 2018).

About the Series

This Cambridge Elements series provides an extensive overview of the many and varied connections between philosophy and logic. Distinguished authors provide an up-to-date summary of the results of current research in their fields and give their own take on what they believe are the most significant debates influencing research, drawing original conclusions.

Cambridge Elements

Philosophy and Logic

Elements in the Series

Set Theory
John P. Burgess

Higher-Order Logic and Type Theory
John L. Bell

A full series listing is available at: www.cambridge.org/EPL

Printed in the United States
by Baker & Taylor Publisher Services